Visual Merchandising

Shirt by Alexander McQueen on 1
Shorts by Marc Jacobs on 1

Shirt by Alexander McQueen on 1
Shorts by Marc Jacobs on 1
Cardigan by Reiss on 1
Plimsoles by Office on 1

Laurence King Publishing

# Visual
# Merchandising

## Window and in-store displays for retail

**Third Edition**

Tony Morgan

**LAURENCE KING**

Published in 2016 by Laurence King
Publishing Ltd in association with the
University of the Arts: London College
of Fashion

Laurence King Publishing Ltd
361–373 City Road
London EC1V 1LR
Tel +44 20 7841 6900
Fax +44 20 7841 6910
Email: enquiries@laurenceking.com
www.laurenceking.com

A catalogue record for this book is
available from the British Library

ISBN 978 178067 687 6

Design concept by Kerrie Powell
This edition designed by Mark Holt

Printed in China

**Front cover**
Selfridges, London.
© Andrew Meredith

**Back cover**
Fortnum & Mason, London.
© Andrew Meredith

**Page 2**
A metallic window scheme entitled
"Mirror Mirror" attracts customers
with its reflective qualities at
Selfridges, London.

# Contents

# Preface

"It is your imagination that needs to be stimulated. Once that happens, the rest is easy. The merchandise is always the leader."

Joe Cotugno, OVP and Creative Director, Bloomingdale's

**If you have ever stood outside a shop admiring the artistry of the window display, been distracted by a sale item while passing through a department store, or paused to take in information from a store guide, then you have been sidetracked by visual merchandising. If you purchased something as a result of stopping in your progress along the pavement or through a store, then you have succumbed to its supremacy.**

For years, the creative individuals who made the stores of the world look appealing for retailers and their loyal customers were known as window dressers or display artists. Display teams had a unique and much-envied function in a store. Occasionally with generous budgets – and most definitely with a huge amount of talent – they mysteriously locked themselves away in studios or lurked behind the curtains of the windows and produced stunning, eye-catching works of art for the shopping community to admire.

During the 1980s, possibly because of a global recession and the threat of e-commerce from the Internet, store bosses suddenly questioned the quantities and abilities of these non-profit-making departments. As a result, they began to push the display artists in-store to cast a creative eye over the racks and rails of discounted merchandise; thus the visual merchandiser was born.

Rarely taken seriously at first because their new roles were unexplained, visual merchandisers were soon laying out departments complete with "sightlines", "focal points" and "hot shops". A new retail vocabulary was born, and soon store interiors had as much sparkle as their windows. Today, visual merchandisers command respect, and are a much sought-after commodity in the retail world as they provide not only a service, but also inspiration and commerciality. This book aims to enlighten and educate students and retailers in the workings of the world of the visual merchandiser. It covers both the art of the window display and in-store visual merchandising and looks at the tools that will help any would-be visual merchandiser succeed.

By using case studies and specially commissioned illustrative diagrams, together with images of the best in window display and in-store interiors from around the world, this book aims to prove how effective visual merchandising can improve a store's brand image and inspire customers to spend.

**Opposite**
A mannequin on a chaise longue reclines at the Rootstein showroom in New York. At a glance, this realistic model looks almost human in appearance.

# The History of Visual Merchandising

**Above**
This fishmonger/poulterer has created
an artistic display of his wares, the
design of which would not look out of
place in the display lore of visual
merchandisers today.

**Below**
In these attention-seeking,
award-winning windows designed
by Thomas Heatherwick for Harvey
Nichols in London, the scheme
explodes through the glass onto
the exterior of the store.

**The first shopkeepers tried to lure consumers into their stores either by ostentatiously exhibiting their names or by displaying products in their windows or on tables in the street, proving that they were open for business and proud of their produce.**

To this day, butchers still fill their windows with fresh meat that serves both as a display to attract customers and also shows the stock of produce available for sale that day. Florists often not only pack their windows with the finest blooms, but trail them outside the store and onto the pavement to entice customers across the threshold using colour and scent. Similarly, barbers will sometimes push a chair with an unsuspecting client up to the glass window in order to prove their skill and popularity.

With the advent of new technology in the 1840s that allowed the production of large panes of glass, department stores were perhaps responsible for taking the art of window display to a higher level, using their large windows as stages, some of them as theatrical as a Broadway show. Today, colour, props and atmospheric lighting on many occasions arrogantly overshadow the merchandise, as visual merchandising extends beyond its role of supporting the wares and becomes an art form, creating a statement and provoking a reaction. Stores like London's Harvey Nichols have collaborated with well-known designers and artists to produce eye-catching schemes where the merchandise becomes part of an artistic work.

Harrods opened in London in 1849 as a small shop selling groceries, perfume and stationery, and grew to become the renowned department store it is today. Mitsukoshi, Tokyo's leading department store, was established even earlier, in 1673, as a kimono specialist. Its innovation was the

**Above**
Bon Marché department store in Paris in the late nineteenth century offered an impressive shopping experience for its customers through the grandeur of its architecture.

**Below**
A Selfridges window from the 1920s shows skill and imagination for its time, with its delicate display of handkerchiefs.

concept of bringing the customer to a store rather than selling from door to door.

It is the department store, with its huge array of merchandise and vast amount of window space, that is the pioneer of the window display. A relatively recent phenomenon, it first began in France. Even there, however, for many years department stores existed only in the capital, Paris. It was Aristide Boucicaut who first had the idea of setting up this kind of store. He wanted to create a shop designed to sell all sorts of merchandise, but also wanted to attract crowds of people who could wander freely about in a little "town within the town". In 1852 Boucicaut opened the world's first department store: Le Bon Marché.

The concept of the department store then spread to the United States, where famous stores as we know them today first opened: Macy's in New York in 1858, Marshall Field's in Chicago in 1865, Bloomingdale's in New York in 1872 and also Wanamaker's in Philadelphia in 1876.

No one retailer or department store can possibly take the credit for producing the first eye-catching staged window display; however, we can certainly look to various individuals who helped set the standards for today's visual merchandisers.

It was American retail entrepreneur Gordon Selfridge who had grand aspirations to bring the concept of the department store – and with it the language of visual merchandising – to Edwardian London. After leaving his post as managing director of the majestic Marshall Field's department store in Chicago and emigrating to England, he arrived in London with great designs to build a long-awaited premier, purpose-built, modern department store.

On 15 March, 1909, Londoners witnessed the unveiling of Gordon Selfridge's £400,000 dream. Selfridges became the benchmark of British retailing. Its vast plate-glass windows were filled with the finest merchandise its proprietor had to offer. Selfridge also revolutionized the world of visual merchandising by leaving the window lights on at night, even when the store was closed, so that the public could still enjoy the presentations while returning home from the theatre.

**Above**
Mitsukoshi, Tokyo, was established in 1673 as a small retailer specializing in kimonos. Today it is Tokyo's leading department store.

Selfridge also included a few innovations in-store for his customers – including a soda fountain for the sociable and a silence room for the less so. He was never one to miss out on a promotional opportunity. When, in July 1909, Louis Blériot crash-landed his aeroplane in a field in Kent after flying across the English Channel, Selfridge had the plane packed on a train at 2 a.m. and on display the same morning at 10 a.m. Fifty thousand people queued to see it that day. By 1928, Selfridges had doubled in size to become the store we now know, due to the hype and success of Gordon Selfridge.

The 1920s saw an explosion of creativity in the arts and fashion, which spilled over into the art of window display, and once again, it was Paris that led the way. Frustrated that their canvases could only be seen in the homes of the rich and famous, many young artists in the city took their skills to the masses. Soon, the arcades of the capital were occupied with Art Deco-inspired themes, and fashion designers now found an innovative and exciting static runway on which to show their creations.

The department stores of New York's Fifth Avenue followed suit. In the 1930s, surrealist artist Salvador Dalí can be credited with setting the American creative criteria in window display. He was approached to dress two windows for the Bonwit Teller store. Street art took on another dimension when he unveiled his "Narcissus" displays, but it was a step too far: his outrageous pastiches were removed after complaints. Yet Dalí's

**Above**
Maybe it is not the most innovative display by today's standards, but Marshall Field's window from the early 1900s caused a public reaction at the time in Chicago.

**Below**
The coats on the mannequins in this 1950s window display at Printemps in Paris may look elegant, but the mannequins are rigid and not grouped to engage with each other.

lack of success did not deter other would-be artists from beginning their careers as window dressers. The artist Andy Warhol began his career in the stores of New York while still at college; Jasper Johns, James Rosenquist and Robert Rauschenberg all worked as window dressers in the 1950s.

It was not only the big department stores that followed the new style of window dressing. As fashion shifted from the couture houses to the high street and social trends developed, fashion designers worldwide began to make the most of their windows. Pierre Cardin, Mary Quant and Vivienne Westwood are just a few who told the youth of yesteryear which social clan they should belong to by dressing their windows to inspire.

Terence Conran was acutely aware of the shifting fashion trends. In 1964, he created a store to match those of the emerging fashion boutiques, but his differed in its type of product: furniture. Chelsea, London, was the epicentre of style and youth culture and Conran was quick to capitalize on this. His first store boasted whitewashed walls, creating a sense of space that came as a revelation to home-owners. Customers who visited his growing empire soon experienced spotlit ceilings, quarry-tile floors and cafés. Nowadays, Habitat still maintains its presence

**Above**
As part of a Rick Owens promotion at Selfridges, London, in 2014, a giant statue of the designer stood in front of the store's iconic façade.

**Above**
The 1960s saw the creation of
high-street ready-to-wear, and Mary
Quant was one of the first designers,
in 1959, to use the window of her
London store as a showcase for her
collections, as well as to promote
social trends.

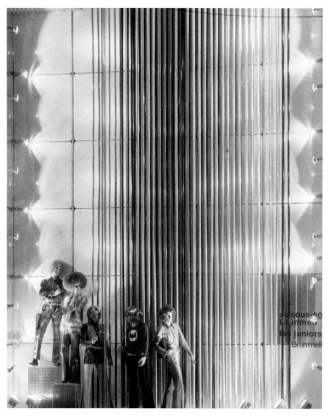

brands were able to produce mass-marketing campaigns that featured the world's most desirable faces and bodies. In the windows of fashion stores, the mannequins that had graciously modelled garments for decades became redundant and were often replaced by huge, glossy-print photographs of emerging catwalk supermodels. Runway shows from the world's fashion capitals were projected on high-tech TV screens, and the clever use of lighting not only enhanced the product, but also helped to create ambience and drama.

Thanks to the experiments and experience of the window dressers from yesteryear, today's visual merchandisers have a lot of proven techniques with which to work. Visual merchandisers working in the proliferating fashion-store chains today, for example, are reintroducing the mannequin to the shop window, having acknowledged it to be a successful option for displaying the latest trends in a similar manner from store to store. The Spanish fashion store Zara, for example, employs traditional window-dressing techniques, its innovative window schemes and clever fashion styling placing its windows alongside those of the major luxury brands.

Now that retail brands have not only taken control of the foremost shopping streets in all major cities but have also infiltrated rural towns and villages, their innovative techniques in visual merchandising have also made an impact on their competitors. In the last decade, brands have pushed the boundaries of visual merchandising not just by creating in-store displays to drive sales and keep the customer inspired, but also by introducing new techniques: DJs performing in urban clothing shops; contemporary eateries flanking fashion floors; books and magazines breaking out of their host departments; and fashion shows that can be viewed not only by the fashionistas but also by lunch-time shoppers.

on the British high street, together with other stores such as Liberty and Harvey Nichols that we sometimes forget paved the way for the retailers of today; in New York an equivalent is Barneys.

The development of technology in the 1990s and the birth of super-brands like Gucci and Prada saw the evolution of window displays into propaganda machines. With massive marketing budgets behind them, these larger

Today, a brand might exist within its own store, but the store can also become a brand in its own right, populating its floor space with other brands, the idea being that together they will generate more sales. This is particularly apparent in the larger department stores like Selfridges, Printemps and Macy's. Either way, the visual merchandiser's task is to communicate a fundamental message to the public through window displays and in-store visual merchandising.

**Above**
By the 1970s, window dressing had begun to reflect the spirit of the age. In this window from Printemps in Paris, the mannequins are displayed in tune with the times, with mirrored plinths suggesting the mirror-balls from the discos of the day.

**Below**
The American fashion brand Banana Republic produces eye-catching window schemes incorporating interesting props, as well as a strong fashion statement, to make their windows both innovative and commercial.

In the twenty-first century, the latest challenge to the supremacy of the traditional store is the Internet. Shopping from home is not only easier but also price-competitive. Stores are under even more pressure to ensure that their customers return and spend, and it is the visual merchandiser who will be key to attracting and retaining their attention. Fortunately, shopping has always been a social activity, and the thrill of it will always be the major part of the consumer experience. Whether shoppers are out to discover an unexpected bargain, find an item sought for a long time or meet up with friends while browsing, it is the job of the retailer to guarantee that they not only purchase but have a positive retail experience. With the help of good visual merchandising, this can easily be achieved.

**Above**
In large department stores, men's designer fashion collections such as those of Givenchy are an important part of the overall brand mix, and are given prime exposure to enhance the brands through excellent product presentation.

# The Role of a Visual Merchandiser

"We are the guys backstage who are stage-managing and producing the whole effect, whereas the buyers are writing the story and providing the content. We are the ones who have to bring it to life."

Alannah Weston, Deputy Chairman, Selfridges

**A visual merchandiser's role is to increase sales: first by attracting shoppers into the store through the power of the window display, and then through in-store display and layout, which needs to encourage them to remain in the store, purchase and have a positive retail experience so that they return.**

Individuals wanting to pursue a career in visual merchandising would benefit from being creative, commercial, understanding and unquestionably hard-working. Long hours, opinionated colleagues and members of the public and tight deadlines are all common challenges that go with the job. In addition, an awareness not only of fashion trends but also of social, political and economic trends would be beneficial for any visual merchandiser. No longer do the fashion pages dictate to the retail world; lifestyle trends are as important as apparel. Where individuals take their

holidays and who they listen to on their iPods may well influence the style and direction of where they choose to shop.

Above all, an unbiased outlook is paramount. A successful store may already have its own winning creative formula, and although the visual merchandising manager may be willing to listen to suggestions, he or she will usually want someone with a commercial mind who can help support the existing team. A non-personal view and unopinionated attitude towards the product you may be asked to work with are necessary. A good visual merchandiser can work with the ugliest and most unsympathetic of products and still come up with great results.

**Above**
The use of dramatically posed mannequins and simple graphics applied to both the wall and floor create a stunning in-store display at Lane Crawford, Hong Kong.

# The day-to-day role of a visual merchandiser

**Depending on whether visual merchandisers work for a large department store, a multi-store retailer or an independent boutique, they will be expected to manage and generally oversee the visual presentation of the windows and in-store displays. This will involve liaising with the buying teams to ascertain what has been bought and how best to promote it. As well as laying out complete floors of new-season merchandise, they will also be expected to set the overall retail standards for the store. Everyday tasks will include ensuring that the fixtures are replenished with the correct product and that the corresponding signage is present, as well as checking that the windows and in-store displays are still presentable, tidy and well-lit.**

Large visual merchandising teams may designate specific roles for individuals to maximize their resources. Individual visual merchandisers working for smaller retailers may be expected not only to dress the windows but arrange for the outside glass to be cleaned regularly. The responsibilities of visual merchandisers seldom stop solely at dressing mannequins.

**Above**
The visual merchandiser puts the finishing touches to the grouping before adjusting the lighting, cleaning the window and inspecting it from outside.

# Training

**Those wishing to enter the profession will usually undertake a visual merchandising course at college or university and then seek work experience in-store, or they can apply directly to a store for work experience.**

There are several visual merchandising courses available. Students are likely to learn how to place products together, create and install windows and merchandise shop floors. Many courses will also give an insight into the advantages of the use of colour, lighting and branding. By using many practical exercises together with theory, these two-year courses give a good insight into the world of visual merchandising and provide the student with a useful and recognized qualification.

Short courses are also offered to would-be store-owners who prefer a fast-track education and may want to learn specific aspects of visual merchandising.

As in many other careers, work experience can be a valuable asset. And in this industry it is common to rely heavily on work-experience students to fill many positions. As Mark Briggs, Creative Director of Saks Fifth Avenue, explains, "Students doing their work placement at Harrods get to cover all aspects of visual merchandising. They get to handle every category of product so that they not only get an understanding of the items but also so they can decide which area they would like to excel in: home, fashion, food or beauty." Briggs develops experts for every product category in the store; a fashion dresser may not necessarily be confident at grouping saucepans, for example.

Young, eager students on work experience – depending on the time of year and the schedule of the visual merchandising team – can find themselves working on a window or sent to clean the stockroom. Either way, their efforts are often recognized, and in a career where visual merchandisers hop from one store to another, positions often become available for those in the right place at the right time. The visual merchandising teams will rely on a full head-count to fulfil their hectic programmes.

## Portfolios

Having a comprehensive portfolio that demonstrates creativity and experience of visual merchandising will undoubtedly help an individual to secure a job in a creative team. An extensive portfolio is also essential in securing freelance work, as it will allow a potential client to ascertain immediately if your skills will benefit their business.

A professional portfolio should contain a collection of images showing examples of current work, printed and presented in a folder or produced digitally and shown on a computer. Many forward-thinking visual merchandisers collate their work on a website that can be accessed using a secure password, so that they can email clients with a link to their portfolio.

It is important to edit a portfolio to suit the job for which you are applying. For example, if a client requires outstanding window displays, the first section of the portfolio should contain examples of window displays. It is vital that the first couple of pages reflect your understanding of the client's requirements. It is also helpful to include examples of other creative skills, such as design software, in-store visual merchandising and branding, as this could encourage more offers of work.

# Visual merchandising in a department store

**Department stores will give a novice excellent training and knowledge of visual merchandising because of the diverse range of products that they house. The training to be gained from an established team is invaluable.**

Traditionally, those entering a visual merchandising team in a department store will begin as dresser or junior visual merchandiser; if they work hard and show that they are willing, they may be promoted within two years to a senior role. Managers are likely to spot potential and develop those they see as future managers by encouraging them to develop their communication and managerial skills, to begin managing a budget and to develop a complete window scheme before they are promoted to a managerial role. Those dressers who enjoy the hands-on practicalities of working on displays may prefer not to pursue a managerial role, given all the administration it involves. A regional department store may have its own visual merchandising team, which takes its lead from the flagship store, but the career path there will be similar to that in the flagship store, with the regional manager controlling the budget and recruitment for the regional store.

Mark Briggs of Harrods recruits most of his 67 staff as students. After completing work experience, they go on to assist him dressing 2 km (1.25 miles) of window space and merchandising 92,903 square metres (1,000,000 sq ft) of shop floor. Mark says that a good structure is key to the smooth running of his team. "Communication is the key word," he explains. "I hold weekly meetings with my team leaders to explain future concepts and promotions to make them feel part of the Harrods family."

Harrods, like many department stores worldwide, employs separate interior and window visual merchandising teams. A visual

merchandiser often has the chance to choose which of the two he or she prefers to excel in; others, however, will be placed according to their merits and talents. Working in both categories will give the trainee visual merchandiser a better overall knowledge and may make the individual more marketable.

**Above**
Oversized gilt picture frames are used as props in this in-store display to create drama and atmosphere at Lane Crawford, Hong Kong.

**Below**
Also at Lane Crawford, these immaculately dressed mannequins interact with homewares to make dramatic in-store displays.

The visual merchandising structure of a typical department store or large multiple retailer is often split into two: the creative team, which plans and designs the window displays, and the visual merchandising team, which oversees the interior of the store or stores.

## Creative director/manager

Responsibilities

To plan and design window schemes.

To negotiate the window production using external prop makers and graphics companies.

To select the correct range of mannequins for each of the window schemes, ensuring that they have relevant wigs and make-up that reflect the fashion trends.

To attend fashion shows, galleries and exhibitions to keep up to date with current fashion and social trends.

To control the creative budget.

To plan each window scheme using an installation calendar.

To manage a team of creative assistants.

## Senior visual merchandise manager/director

Responsibilities

To establish and oversee the creative look of the store.

To liaise with the buying director to ensure that the correct product is promoted.

To work closely with the operation director to guarantee that the store layouts are planned correctly.

To communicate with the marketing director to make certain that the visual merchandising team supports any store product promotions.

To control a payroll and visual merchandising budget.

To purchase relevant props and mannequins.

To recruit qualified staff.

To manage the store's graphics and signage.

## Visual merchandise manager

Responsibilities

To manage a team.

To liaise with buyers and marketing.

To communicate with the senior visual merchandise manager.

To design and implement in-store and window displays.

To interact with the graphics team.

To liaise with floor managers.

To know competitors.

To communicate with brands.

## Senior visual merchandiser

Responsibilities

To mentor junior members of the team.

To act as a bridge between visual merchandise manager and floor manager.

To be aware of fashion trends and key looks.

To maintain retail standards.

To communicate with the graphics team.

To educate shop-floor staff.

To work closely with brands to ensure a consistent product representation.

## Junior/dresser visual merchandiser

Responsibilities

To maintain retail standards.

To be aware of fashion trends.

To work closely with shop-floor staff to ensure visual guidelines are met.

To understand and be aware of brands.

To present merchandise both creatively and with the maximization of sales in mind.

## Carpenters

A carpenter's role within a department store is not just confined to the making of props in the studio; he or she will be instrumental in installing and removing windows and in-store displays. Fully qualified and professionally trained carpenters will also know when a prop needs to be finished to a high standard because it may be placed where the public will scrutinize it up close, and when to compromise on overall quality because it may only be viewed from the front and through glass. Carpenters working in a visual merchandising team will often be able to extend their talents beyond working in wood and will be able to make props from a variety of media.

## Painters

Apart from the obvious – painting windows – a painter working in a visual merchandising team may offer a variety of skills. Many are experts in paint effects, and – in conjunction with the carpenters – will be responsible for applying the finishing touches to eye-catching props and window schemes.

## Prop makers

Props are an essential ingredient in an eye-catching window. Every successful visual merchandiser will have some experience of using tools and materials to create and install a window or in-store display, but experienced prop makers can produce outstanding bespoke props to a higher, more professional standard. With shop-floor space becoming more valuable, many department stores and large multiple retailers have closed their in-store prop studios, and now outsource the work. Working to a budget and a brief presented by the store's creative team, the prop maker will present their initial concepts, which may be amended to suit the budget. The props can then be built externally months in advance. Often the prop maker will also be employed to install their work under the guidance of the visual merchandising team.

### Porters

It may seem a luxury to employ porters. However, ensuring that valuable furniture and exquisite props enter and leave the windows in one piece is essential. Most porters will also be responsible for managing and maintaining the stockroom that houses props and mannequins.

### Graphic designers

In-house graphics teams are now slowly being disbanded in favour of outside agencies that provide not only the ideas, but also the equipment and skill to create a store's artwork. The benefits of an in-house graphics team are, however, unquestionable. Unlike outside contractors, its members will be aware of the store's overall image and, undoubtedly, having them on hand to produce samples that can be edited on-site saves a lot of valuable time. In or out of house, a graphics team is responsible for the consistent application of the store's graphic design to price tickets, banners and promotional information.

### Online visual merchandisers

The presentation of products to the customer is now important not only in a store but also online. Retailers employ individuals to manage the appearance of their websites so that they are easy to navigate and purchase from. An online visual merchandiser will liaise with the buying teams to ensure that the latest products are easily identifiable at the click of a mouse. They may work with the text editors responsible for writing product descriptions, and because of the speed and accessibility of the Internet, they will be able to manage markdowns and seasonal offers, communicating them accurately and immediately to their customers.

An online visual merchandising team is often responsible for the styling of the products. Next employs a team of photographers to shoot each item in the company's in-house studio, retouching them and uploading them to the website within hours. Some retailers expect the manufacturer to provide professional images that they can upload without any studio or model costs.

**Above**
Paint tins and brushes as props complement brightly coloured hosiery in this "Colourist" window theme, which involved Selfridges' (London) whole visual merchandising team, from managers to graphic designers.

# Visual merchandising of multiple chain stores

Many high-street multiple chain stores have a creative team to design, plan and organize their window displays. They then tell the visual merchandising teams when and how the window schemes should be installed, and offer tips on mannequin dressing and styling. High-street chains will have a similar visual merchandising structure to that of a department store. However, each store may not have the luxury of its own in-house visual merchandiser. Instead, one visual merchandiser or a team of visual merchandisers may travel from store to store in a chain, covering specific areas of the country. For any major promotions such as Christmas and sales, other visual merchandisers may be drafted in to help. However, visual merchandising is usually undertaken by just one individual. Working for an area manager, the visual merchandiser in a multiple chain will be recruited through the firm's head office and will then follow a career path similar to that of a visual merchandiser in a department store.

These positions are best suited to organized individuals who enjoy travelling – even travelling abroad as, on many occasions, the stores for which they are responsible are overseas. Of course, those working for a chain whose head office is overseas may also have to travel to that office for briefings.

**Above**
The floor layout at this Zara store in Salamanca, Spain, was carefully planned. A display of mannequins and folded products acts as an anchor, or focal point, in the centre, while sufficient space has been left around it for customers to circulate.

A visual merchandiser working for a multiple high-street chain will be given guidance and direction from the company's head office. There the visual merchandising manager will design and plan the installation of windows and in-store visual merchandising projects for the entire chain, and will then filter the tasks through to the individual area visual merchandisers. International stores, such as Gap, follow these rules. The Gap head office in the USA, for example, enforces strict guidelines to ensure that the brand is not compromised. It communicates brand strategy and visual guidelines to visual merchandising managers in each of the countries in which Gap has a store, who then delegate tasks to the relevant members of their team.

Guidelines may include a plan of how the store's linear space (wall space) should be merchandised, produced using either Adobe Photoshop or InDesign with illustrated templates or photographs of the product. The in-house visual merchandising team will stipulate whether the products should be folded or hung, and how they should be placed together to build outfits. Outfit building involves the placing together of specific merchandise to create an entire look; for example, a shirt, pair of trousers and a jacket, which may be displayed with accessories, encouraging the customer to purchase the whole seasonal trend.

The store's head office may produce a similar pack to demonstrate how the whole shop floor should be arranged. This will include the repositioning of fixtures for seasonal collections. During sale times the visual merchandising teams will be given clear instructions about where items should be placed to create maximum sales impact.

All these guidelines are sent to the in-store and area visual merchandise teams in a printed pack, or via email so that they can be implemented immediately.

The flagship store in a chain – usually the largest and most prominent – often has the most elaborate window displays. Because they often vary in size, individual regional stores will have window schemes tailor-made to suit the size of the windows. Budgetary constraints may also mean that they rely on more economical and simpler window schemes, such as print-work that may form a backdrop for the product, which can be installed by just one visual merchandiser.

Communication is paramount for a visual merchandiser in a multiple chain store, as he or she has to ensure that all of the stores launch the same product in their windows at the same time. Promotional activities will also require coordination and planning.

The day-to-day role of a multiple chain store visual merchandiser will include communicating the visual strategy to each of the store managers and store staff, one of whom will be expected to maintain any in-store and window displays. Signage and ticketing can be ordered and monitored by the visual merchandiser also.

**Above**
A group of mannequins strike dramatic poses under a ceiling covered with metallic branding in this Topshop store in Liverpool, UK. The surrounding area has been merchandised with the current trends, as seen on the mannequins.

# Visual merchandising of small retail outlets

**Smaller independent shops may enlist the help of a self-employed visual merchandiser to help promote their merchandise. "Freelancers", as they are often called, can change the look and atmosphere of a store in a matter of hours. Because they generally work on a project-fee basis, freelancers are usually fast and efficient. Most of these creative individuals have trained within an established and renowned visual team and have contacts who can manufacture props and signage for them. A freelancer may specialize in designing windows or in in-store visual merchandising, or may offer both services. Some may also specialize in fashion styling, while others may excel at product grouping. It is always best to ask to see freelancers' portfolios before engaging them, as these will contain examples of their work.**

Most freelancers find their work by word of mouth; a stunning window acts as a good marketing tool not only for the store, but also for its creator. Clearly the more skilled and efficient freelancers are, the more work they may acquire.

On some occasions an independent store-owner will spot the creative potential in a member of staff and encourage him or her to dress the windows and arrange the in-store displays. With no formal training, this can be risky: not only will the makeshift visual merchandiser have no mentor to learn from, he or she may also pick up bad habits that will not transfer well into a reputable visual merchandising team in the future. In the smaller retail outlet, arranging for a member of staff to attend a short course in visual merchandising would be beneficial.

**Above**
Last Footwear, an independent store in Brighton, UK, has been designed using pieces of second-hand furniture and accessories. The ladder used for displaying the belts is highly effective.

# Measuring success

**It is not always easy to gauge the success of a window display or the effectiveness of an in-store display. Despite the hard work that visual merchandisers may put in, retailers can be competitive within their own stores. A well-presented window may create overwhelming sales, for which the buyers may take the credit, attributing the success to the products they selected. However, a window that performs badly will undoubtedly be blamed on the visual merchandiser.**

In the overall scheme, it is important for retailers to realize that changing the window display may not generate sudden sales, and that the long-term effect of how the brand is evolving through the use of consistently good windows and in-store displays is more important. Quick wins can often be achieved; however, a structured, achievable plan –

which may include advance preparation and allocation of personnel set against the budget – is more realistic in ensuring that sales and the reputation and image of the store grow as a result of the visual merchandising. Forming a professional relationship with the buyers and shop-floor staff will undoubtedly help visual merchandisers prove their worth and expertise. Together they should be able to share the success of the store's visual merchandising.

**Above**
In Colette, Paris, simple but effective
bust forms are dressed to inspire and
inform the customers of the latest
seasonal trends. The collections
are strategically placed close by.

# Store Design

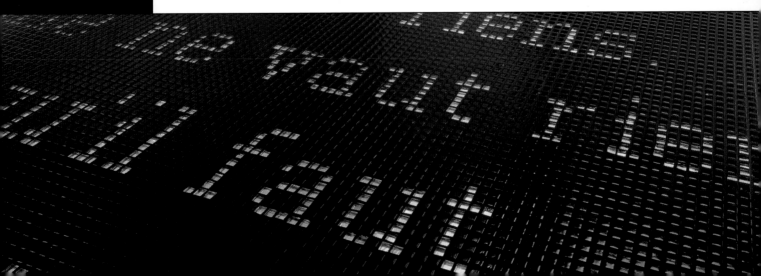

# What is store design?

**Various department stores worldwide have been moulded into amazing show-stopping retail emporia. With their grand façades, Harrods in London – whose thousands of lightbulbs glow like a shopper's paradise – and Samaritaine, once Paris's largest department store, have always stood the test of time. With the invention of visual merchandising during the 1980s, however,** **retailers saw the necessity of offering its customers the same experience in-store. Store design became crucial to success. Today, many designer outlets in particular spend as much time and investment on their store's design as on their collections.**

Store design unites all aspects of visual merchandising: window display and interior design as well as fixtures and fittings and lighting. Visual merchandisers, architects and interior designers have always worked hand in hand to create retail environments that are inspirational yet commercial and above all, a canvas on which visual merchandisers can demonstrate their skills. It would be sense-less for an architect to develop a store's interior without first understanding the visual merchandiser's needs and requirements. A good store design will show products to their best advantage. Walkways, lighting and signage are all major features that need to be discussed even before the important fixtures are designed. Some retailers may also enlist the help of interior decorators, lighting designers and artists to help create the in-store ambience.

**Above**
The architects of the Prada store in New York, Rem Koolhaas's OMA (Office for Metropolitan Architecture), did not stop at just providing a back-drop for the merchandise; they also created a retail space that can be converted into a performance space at the touch of a button. The ramp that opens up to reveal a stage for performances is situated opposite a fixed seating area, creating a sense of theatre and providing an ambience to attract customers to the store.

**Below**
Great care and attention has clearly been given to the lighting in this store for Alexander McQueen in Milan, designed by William Russell. Lighting is completely concealed in the ceiling and along the perimeter walls, with all plugs, lightbulbs and unsightly grilles hidden. A pillar with a surrounding seat anchors the whole space and is used as a centrepiece for movement around the floor, while muted light colours provide an easy backdrop for any fashion collection.

# Why is store design important?

**The design of a store can help support the brand image as well as underpin a successful retail strategy. Retailers rely on the design of the store to entice customers inside. While some retailers prefer a more subtle store design, others like to shock and inspire, creating stores that generate hype and discussion.**

Before choosing which road to go down, a retailer should first consider the demographics of its customers. Traditional shoppers would possibly not be impressed if their local department store turned futuristic and contemporary. Most multiple retailers have a proven set format that they use when opening stores. Established retailers such as Britain's Marks & Spencer would perhaps suffer if they unexpectedly designed an avant-garde store; the risk would be too high and might unnerve their loyal following. There are times, however, when it may be advantageous to break the mould. In September 2003, for example, Selfridges embraced a more contemporary outlook and departed from the turn-of-the-twentieth-century style of its Oxford Street building in London when it opened a futuristic-style store in Birmingham, England. The building was part of the rejuvenation of the city's 1960s Bullring shopping centre. With hundreds of silver discs adorning the blue organic shell, the new store is either loathed or loved by the locals, but, as Gordon Selfridge would have appreciated, at least it is noticed and opinions are formed.

Some retailers will invest more money in their flagship stores. A flagship store is usually situated on a busy shopping street, where it will attract the most customers. Oxford Circus in London boasts the best flagship stores in the country, with the likes of Topshop, Nike and H&M taking up prime space. A flagship store will also have a larger budget for window displays and a wider selection of merchandise because of its greater floor space. Many have a dedicated visual merchandising team that sets the standards for the rest of the chain's stores nationwide.

**Above**
Future Systems' design for the Birmingham Selfridges, UK, which opened in 2003, has become an iconic part of the city's architecture. Like the flagship store on London's Oxford Street, it does not have its name emblazoned across the entrance. Gordon Selfridge himself said that the store didn't need a name – everyone would know the building by its very design – and the new store in Birmingham follows the precedent in spectacular style.

# Who designs the store?

At some time all retailers will have to consult with an architect, either to design a new store, renovate an existing one or rejuvenate an area of their shop. Normally, they will consult an architect experienced in commercial practice, which differs from domestic architecture due to the need to take public access into consideration. On most occasions, retailers will choose architects with experience in store design because of their knowledge and proven track record. Others, however, may challenge young talented designers to create their stores.

In designing stores, many architects will add their signature style, which more often than not is why they were commissioned in the first place. When the famous French crystal manufacturer Baccarat approached the noted designer and architect Philippe Starck to

**Above**
IT Beijing Market is as impressive at night as it is during the day, with clever lighting and innovative graphics.

design its headquarters in Paris, the directors must have foreseen that his opulent yet quirky creation would create waves among their existing loyal customers. To enforce his design, Starck also created an exclusive collection of crystal for sale in the store.

Before starting on the store design, the more information the architect is given about the product and the brand, the easier it will be to understand the task. An architect needs to be aware of the product items to be sold and the stock densities for each fixture, because fixtures need to be functional as well as part of an overall design concept. Product adjacencies are also key in creating a cohesive floor, and of course the all-important cash desks, stockrooms and offices need to be incorporated in the final design, all of which are part of the remit of the visual merchandiser (see page 120).

**Above**
Here Philippe Starck has created a juxtaposition of free-standing modern cabinets against the backdrop of a traditional-style fresco, which is sympathetic to the style of the Baccarat collection.

An architect will start by preparing concept ideas for the client to approve; the initial ideas will seldom be what may have been expected. Once the designs have been approved, the architect will produce floor plans and a timeline of how the overall building work will be completed, as well as the ever-important budget. The architect will also suggest building contractors and specialists to build the shop fit and will manage and oversee the whole process. Contractors will include builders, electricians, painters and carpenters. Between them lies the responsibility to ensure that the deadline for the store opening is met.

**Above**
Water and electricity don't usually mix, yet here in Maison Baccarat's store in Paris, Starck has suspended a lit chandelier in a contemporary aquarium, creating a quirky yet stunning visual.

# Pop-up shops

**Pop-up shops have been popular since the turn of the twenty-first century. They started as a marketing tool to increase brand identity outside the retailer's traditional surroundings. A pop-up shop, as the name suggests, appears for a limited time in a temporary space. Many retailers take advantage of derelict premises in prime locations or use mobile units, such as shipping containers.**

Gucci launched a pop-up shop selling just trainers in a disused store in Covent Garden, London. It received a lot of media attention, which no doubt increased awareness and confirmed the brand's street credibility and reputation for innovation. In 2011 the businessman Roger Wade opened BOXPARK in trendy Shoreditch, east London. This collection of refitted shipping containers forms an urban pop-up shopping mall

**Above**
Launched in 2011 in London's trendy East End, BOXPARK is a collection of retailers trading from recycled shipping containers.

consisting not only of fashion brands but also of lifestyle stores and cafés. The whole concept is in keeping with the ethos of Shoreditch's vibrant multicultural community. The people of Buenos Aires, meanwhile, woke one morning to discover a huge Adidas shoebox in the centre of town with the lid half open. This pop-up store received huge media attention across the globe. Even the online trader eBay opened its first bricks-and-

mortar store in the form of a temporary pop-up shop.

**Above**
To coincide with rap star Kanye West's New York shows, he opened a one-off pop-up shop selling his Yeezus merchandise.

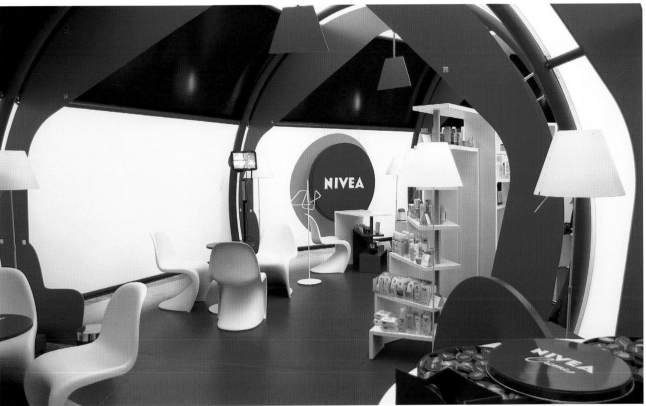

**Above and below**
The pop-up Nivea lab, which appeared
in the centre of Milan to the
amusement of locals, not only
promoted Nivea products but also
included a hairdresser.

# How does store design work?

**The main purpose of store design is to show a product to its best advantage. This is achieved through a combination of ambience, functionality and an inviting design. Each store will be different, depending on its product; a supermarket will be more concerned with functionality, while a retailer of luxury goods will be more concerned about creating the right atmosphere.**

Independent store-owners can take the risk of promoting more adventurous store design. Some of the most imaginative designs can be found in Japan. The streets of Tokyo hide many interesting retail outlets, the most exciting of which are hidden in the back streets instead of taking centre stage on the main shopping thoroughfares. The four small overcrowded islands, thousands of kilometres from the West, are a melting pot of creativity. Small spaces are transformed into retail galleries. The Sony Centre in the Ginza region of Tokyo is an interactive techno-shopper's emporium: floors of the latest gadgets and software are available for customers to sample; plasma screens cover ceilings, and interactive information demonstrates innovative ideas.

A Bathing Ape in Japan primarily sells casual clothes and fashion accessories displayed in Perspex racks mounted on a glass floor that offers a view of the basement. The brand has achieved cult status not only in Japan but also worldwide because of its quirky product and store design.

Offering a complete contrast in terms of space, the iconic British brand Burberry opened its flagship store in 2012 on Regent Street, London, in the shell of the cinema where Queen Victoria watched her first film. (The building has also been a church and meat market.) Burberry's Chief Creative Director and Executive Officer, Christopher Bailey, fused technology with physical product to create an interactive fashion emporium with 3D hologram fashion shows, interactive iPads and free Wi-Fi for loyal customers. The marriage of old and new design makes the store an inviting prospect, with its fascinating insight into London's Victorian past.

Milan's Corsa Como has attracted the world's fashion pack for years. It is hidden away at the end of an unassuming walkway, but the customer's first impression on entering the store is the vast scale of the space. An alfresco dining area fills the courtyard and then branches onto the retail area and a restaurant. Stairs lead to a bookshop and finally to an exhibition space on the first floor. The fixtures are not the most costly or innovative – most of them were at some stage retro pieces of furniture or lighting – but positioned together, they create a unique selling environment. Not all store designs need vast budgets; resourceful and interesting schemes often make the most exciting shops.

**Above**
The famous ladies' shoe department at Saks Fifth Avenue, New York, has been designed using subtle, neutral colours and metallics so that the products stand out. An impressive installation of crystals hangs from the ceiling, creating drama.

# Store study:
# Kurt Geiger

**Rebecca Farrar-Hockley is the buying and creative director for luxury shoe brand Kurt Geiger. Not only does Kurt Geiger own several independent UK stores, the company also has prominent concessions in Harrods, Selfridges and other major department stores, including La Rinascente in Milan. The new flagship store in London's Covent Garden was designed by visual merchandising and display consultant John Field, along with the architectural firm Found Associates, with whom Kurt Geiger has collaborated successfully in the past.**

Rebecca Farrar-Hockley, John Field and chief executive officer of Found Associates, Richard Found, discuss the key issues of designing a store and their expectations for the visual merchandising.

## On the subject of designing a store with visual merchandising in mind for Kurt Geiger

Rebecca Farrar-Hockley (RFH) "Shoe shops present an enormous challenge for designers and visual merchandisers because the whole presentation is about display. Customers do not shop the same way for shoes as they do for clothes because they cannot help themselves to the product and simply take it straight to the cash desk; you cannot have every size available on-shelf, and often the product is too expensive to leave unattended. In effect, the whole shop is like a large window display. Clearly the correct visual presentation can affect overall sales; there should be no room for human error. It is important that Kurt Geiger shops are designed in a way that means they need little dressing. Because of the number of stores we have, it can be hard to maintain them effectively. An easy, foolproof store design suits us best."

## On the collaboration between retailer and designer

Richard Found (RF) "We always ask clients for a detailed written brief because it will force them to think about requirements and needs. It then helps us to bring more sustenance in providing the answers."

RFH "It is so important that both parties have a strong professional relationship. With all our projects, Richard has understood the complications of our shoe business and is fully aware of the brand image we want to promote."

**Above**
Mirrored ceilings reflect the dramatically positioned mannequins seated below.
The use of glass helps to give the impression of space.

**Above**
Backlit shelves help to draw the customer's eye to the products, while the use
of mirrors makes the store appear larger.

### On stock densities

RF "It is important to understand just how much product the store is required to show. It would be pointless designing a store that is beautiful yet impractical."

RFH "Future growth is also important and needs to be taken into consideration. I have to grow sales and make sure I make a good turnover. In the future, I might need to introduce more products that will eat into the valuable sales floor."

RF "It becomes a kaleidoscope. When customers pass, it changes perspective and creates movement."

### On fixture requirements

RF "Three or four tried-and-tested fixture configurations are the main proven requirements that will produce good results. There would be no point [in] altering the shelf

heights that work so well in other stores, for example."

RFH "When working for another retailer, I once merchandised a department that had been designed with many extra fixture components, supposedly made to support the visual merchandising. I found, however, that the fixtures were sufficient by themselves because the product was visually very strong, so the extra components were not needed. Good fixtures blend into the background, allowing the products to stand out."

### On key features

John Field (JF) "In the Covent Garden store we wanted to add a key feature: a 'shoe chandelier' at the top of the main mirrored staircase that also reflected beautifully into the mirrored ceiling. This was constructed in stainless steel and Perspex from a specialist company in west London normally known for

**Above left**
Mannequins are positioned on large steps, drawing the customer down to the lower ground floor. The display not only adds theatre to the store but also acts as a strong focal point of the selling space.

**Above right**
A shoe chandelier made up of 200 "must-have" shoes sits at the top of the mirrored staircase: a true fashion statement that enforces the brand's concept.

customized staircases. The chandelier holds 200 shoes circling the lines of Paulmann tube lamps dimmed down to a warm internal glow."

## On the use of colour

RF "A relatively blank canvas for the products to sit within will give you stronger flexible options. Strong-coloured walls may clash with colourful shoes."

JF "Texture added to the materials used enriches the quality of the shoes as well as adding more flexibility to present the ranges in segmented formats and different combinations. We can use Plexiglas, red lava stone and mirror-polished stainless steel for the shinier stilettos, while using sandblasted timbers and industrial felts for the more earthy and urban styles."

## On lighting

RF "All aspects of design are crucial. If you fail in one thing, you can fail at everything. Lighting is one of the most fundamental aspects of design. Bad lighting can change the appearance of the product; a yellow light on brown leather can turn the shoe red. Lighting that emits a white light will give a more accurate overall effect."

## On brand identity

RFH "I prefer to have a thread or common element that is synonymous with Kurt Geiger, rather than an identical format for every shop."

RF "The size and position of the store may also dictate what you can achieve with the design concept. The Covent Garden shop is part of a historic run of listed buildings. The design process includes many legal implications and building requirements."

**Above**
The two red sofas are strong visual elements that sit adjacent to a wall of backlit shoes. The seating is not only visually aesthetic but practical.

**Below**
Stands that not only elevate the shoes but that are designed to show the shoes at a 45-degree angle are helpful in promoting individual styles.

# Windows

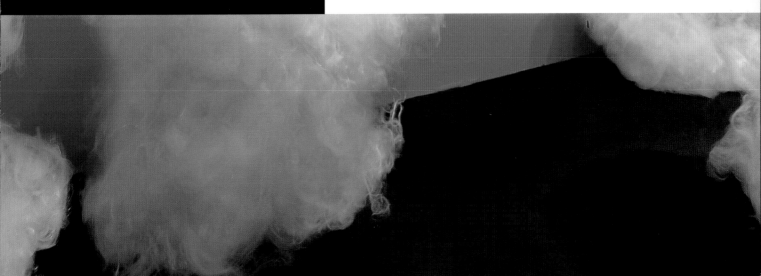

"If Selfridges were a magazine,
the windows would be the front cover."

Alannah Weston, Deputy Chairman, Selfridges

**carefully planned. A well-dressed window display not only attracts shoppers into the store, it also enforces the retailer's brand image. It can act as an advertising tool and give an insight into what is available in-store.**

Depending on the type of store, different factors will drive the make-up of the window display at different times, and consequently the amount of creative licence allowed to the visual merchandiser. A large department store (or even a small retail outlet) may wish to attract attention to its store by creating a display with a noteworthy theme intended to cause a reaction. This type of window is less likely to be driven by product alone; it is steered instead by the marketing or buying department anxious to promote a particular product or trend into which they have bought heavily or wanting to front an advertising campaign. A product-driven window can be used equally in a department store or small retail outlet, but it is more likely to be the main type of window in a multiple chain store, where the need to reach the mass market is particularly vital.

Whatever the driving force behind the window display, there are a number of considerations to be taken into account when planning the window, including the type of window, the best way to group products, whether or not to introduce a theme or scheme and the use of props, lighting, graphics and signage.

**There is no doubt that windows can be used to sell if they are eye-catching and innovative. They are the only major marketing tool that you do not have to pay for because they are part of the store's architecture, apart from the initial set-up costs, so it is worth making the most of them. Many retailers still spend a vast amount of their marketing budget creating works of art; others present their products simply, yet effectively. Some, however, never use their windows to their full capacity. Whether a window is large – similar to that of a department store – or simply a modest-sized one looking into a store, each needs to be**

**Above**
Selfridges' "Future Punk" window scheme features a contemporary view of the punk era. Neon lighting and brightly coloured mannequins were the main theme running throughout the London store.

**Opposite**
These windows consist of simple lines and bold colourful "Shapes" to promote a revival of the 1960s fashion look.

# Getting to know your windows

**Before attempting to design and dress a window, it is best to understand the space and depth of the window you might be expected to work with, as well as the practical features that will affect what you can put into the window and how.**

### Window size and style

The scale of the window you have to work with may affect what you can achieve. There is no standard size or shape of window in the high street; every store window will differ. Larger windows will require a lot more merchandise and more props to fill them; others may require less. In addition to the scale of the window, there are a variety of styles. The most common of are closed, open-back and showcase windows. Thought also needs to be given to shops with no window at all.

### Closed windows

These are usually seen in department stores. With a large pane of glass at the front (facing the audience in the street), a solid back wall and two solid side walls and a door, these windows resemble a room. They are the most thrilling to dress because you can capture the public's attention from just one angle: the street.

Closed windows need considerable planning before they are dressed. Usually large, they will require a lot of merchandise to fill them. Props will also have to be big, and possibly made in multiples, thus adding to the cost. However, expensive merchandise can be used, providing that the door is secure and customers will not be able to gain access and tamper with the presentation. From a design point of view, because they are seen from only one angle, the dressing needs only to be front-facing.

### Open-back windows

These have no back wall but may have side walls. Many retailers prefer them because they make the interior of the shop visible from the outside. This does mean, however, that the interior will need to be maintained and look attractive at all times. These windows can be more difficult to dress because they are viewed from both outside and inside. Unlike in the closed window, expensive merchandise would not be secure, so it is not suitable for use in this type of window. Thought also needs to be given to the possibility that customers may be able to touch the display.

### No window

Shopping arcades often have good examples of stores with no windows. The whole front of the store is exposed to the public with only a grille to separate the store from the public in the evening. Because there is no door or partition stopping customers from entering, these stores encourage the public to walk inside and browse. There may seem to be no window-display requirement; however, display bases can be positioned just inside the entrance with presentations dressed to attract the customers.

**Above**
A closed window can be treated like a stage, as shown here at Selfridges, London, where the window scheme faces the audience – the passing shopper on the street.

**Below**
Like a closed window, open-back windows should be dressed towards the customer on the street, but because they give a view into the store, both the window and the store sides need to be well maintained. This example shows Stella McCartney, New York.

### Corner windows

Here, the windows wrap around a corner. In these windows groupings should be dressed towards the centre of the arc. Clever use of groupings can help lead the customer from one side of the window all the way around to the other and on towards the entrance of the store.

### Arcade windows

Here, the door is set back from the windows. In this case, part of the display should be facing the pavement to gain the customer's attention, and another part of it should be set on the return, leading the customer towards the door.

### Angled windows

These are angled back to the entry. This type of window is gradually being replaced on the high street, but if you are faced with such a window, remember that groupings and products should be displayed parallel to the pane of glass – not to the pavement or sidewalk. This is because customers are more likely to stop and stand in front of the pane of glass on their journey towards the door. Dressing a window in this way gives you the advantage of being able to work with the whole surface area of the glass.

### Showcase windows

Stores that specialize in small items such as jewellery often rely on showcase windows to attract the customer's attention. These miniature windows are placed at eye level to allow close scrutiny of the merchandise.

**Above left**
The entrance to a store with arcade windows is farther away from the street; the role of window dressing here is to draw the customer along the window and into the store, as is the case with Max Studio, Los Angeles.

**Above right**
A corner window will attract attention from two angles. It is therefore important to ensure that both windows are eye-catching – as are these in Bershka, San Sebastian, Spain.

**Below left**
Positioned at eye level, the showcase is the perfect place in which to present smaller, more precious items, as demonstrated at Cartier in Selfridges, London.

## Window set-up

Before designing a window, the visual merchandiser needs to understand what is available to work with. Ideally, an experienced visual merchandiser would like a blank canvas to work on that has certain features.

### Solid wooden walls

A closed window will always benefit from having strong, solid walls. The back wall forms a backdrop to the window display. Together with the side walls, it should have an even surface that can be painted or covered to coordinate with the window scheme. All the walls should also be strong enough to take nails or screws.

### Floor panels

MDF removable floor panels are easy to take out and cover, either with fabrics or PVC. They can also hold nails and screws. Being able to alter the flooring in a window can dramatically change the whole appearance of the presentation. Some smaller retailers prefer a fixed floor that is painted every time the scheme changes, while others may prefer a solid, fixed wooden or stone floor that is not altered each time the window is dressed. Both are acceptable but need to be taken into consideration when planning the window scheme. A solid stone floor will not be suitable for striking a mannequin because it may not be possible to hammer a nail into such a dense surface (see page 211).

### Ceiling grid

A sturdy metal grid painted the same colour as the ceiling so that it blends in is of the utmost importance in any window; you may want to hang banners, props or even mannequins from it at some time. In the longer term, it will mean that holes don't have to be made in the walls for screws and bolts, necessitating repair work before the next dressing.

### Secure door

In a closed window, a concealed door will not only enable you to enter and exit the window, it will also secure any expensive products. Ideally a door in a closed window is best positioned on a side wall rather than the back wall, where it would dominate the window display and would be in full view of the customers. A good-quality locking device is also recommended.

If you are working on a particularly tall window, mannequins can be elevated on plinths to help fill the larger space.

**Above**
Three sporty mannequins run and jump through the Nike window in Beijing, China. Their dramatic poses enforce the brand's concept. Using only red merchandise reflects the Nike logo.

Sculpture by Benoît Ageron

A contemporary young French sculptor who creates both abstract and figurative work in welded steel and raw wood. His work interprets the relationships of man and nature and how one influences other. His artistic approach is a permanent quest of shapes, expressions and movements.

GIVENCHY

www.pariscalling.org.uk

### Lighting tracks

Many of the greatest windows are made even more eye-catching by the clever use of lighting. This is only possible if the window is equipped with high-quality lighting fixtures. We will explore lighting requirements later in the book (see page 98).

### Electrical outputs

It is advantageous to have a few plug sockets in any window. They should be hidden either side of the window next to the glass. As with the door, customers should not be able to spot the sockets on the back wall. It is also wise to install a couple in the ceiling close to the glass and out of sight.

### Window blind

Many visual merchandisers prefer to create their masterpieces while hidden from the public. A window blind also hides the mess caused while either dressing or stripping a window.

### Easy access

Moving larger props or furniture items into a window will be much easier if the door is wide enough. The visual merchandiser also needs access to be able to manoeuvre items through the department at the back of the window.

### Speakers

In many department or large stores, security is paramount. While a visual merchandiser may be locked away dressing a window, it is important that he or she keeps in contact with the outside world via in-store announcements.

### Fire sprinklers

Fires have been known to start in a window because of faulty wiring or an overheated light fitting. A fully operational sprinkler system will help prevent such accidents.

**Above**
Painted the same colour as the ceiling, the lighting grid can be used to hold the lighting tracks, as well as props and products as shown.

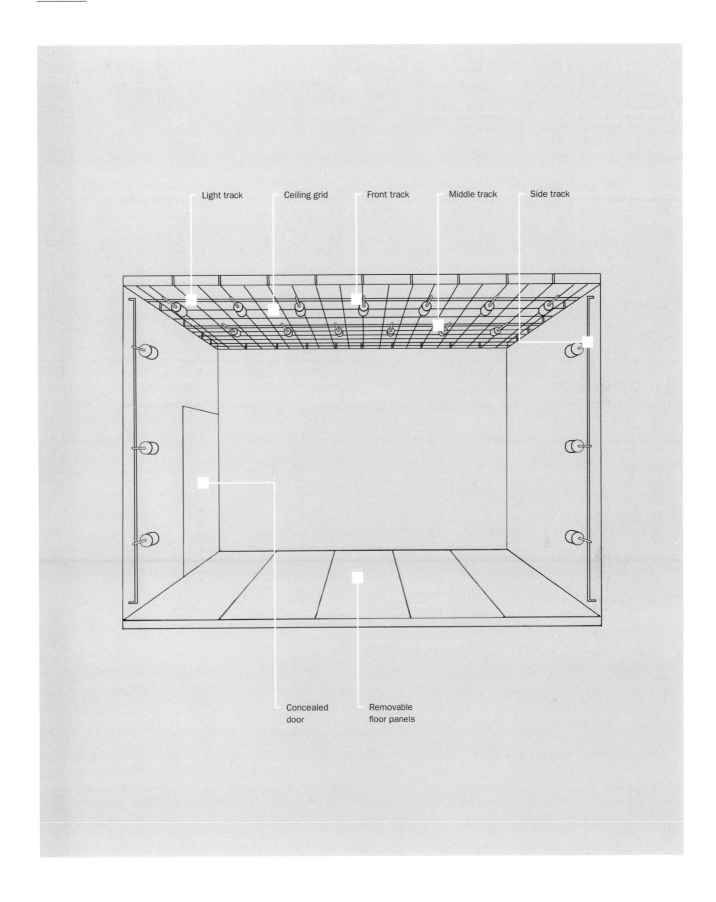

Light track   Ceiling grid   Front track   Middle track   Side track

Concealed
door

Removable
floor panels

**Above**
With all the correct components for a
window in place, the display will be
ready for installation.

# Planning a window display

"The first step when designing a window is to define a theme and the spirit in which you want to put things forward. Then, you have to find THE idea: that very special idea that will make the difference visually."

Franck Banchet, Creative Director, Printemps

**Once you are familiar with your canvas – your window – you can then start to plan your display. At this point you also need to consider what you are aiming to achieve with your display. Are you aiming to shock, attract or cause a buzz, as large department stores such as Barneys in New York or Harvey Nichols in London have done? There are numerous reasons why a visual merchandiser will choose to design a window in a particular way, but first and foremost he or she must ensure that the window theme reflects or is sympathetic to the products being sold in-store.**

Window displays will often take the form of a story, incorporating other elements or props (see pages 68–73) that either have something in common with the merchandise or may be completely unrelated but still maintain an artistic balance between props and product. Some retailers like to treat their customers with windows that show no merchandise, yet sell the image of the store or an event occurring in-store; pieces of art, live performances and animated sets have been used successfully in this way. During sale times it is not uncommon to use merchandise alone to create a window display. With all of these factors in mind, the visual merchandiser will then consider which option is best for a particular project.

**Above**
In this "politically correct" window composed of graphics and a mannequin, Topshop in London ensures that its customers understand that it does not sell real fur. It gets its message across by using cuddly toys to create a fake fur coat.

**Above**

Windows need not always be used to promote any specific product. They can be designed to stop passing potential customers in their tracks, as with this window in Printemps, Paris, where dancers perform live in the window.

**Below**

When British pop group Florence + the Machine was asked to design a window for Selfridges, London, its members drew inspiration from their hit, "Between Two Lungs". Here, a mannequin lies with neon lungs on display to the public.

Creating a window display that will have an emotional yet thought-provoking effect on customers is not always easy. Alannah Weston from Selfridges, London, believes that the execution and the language of a display are vital. "Brilliant execution is at the heart of good window display," she says. "Not having too many ideas, having a great composition and really being able to tell a story are so important when designing a window display. Here at Selfridges we are lucky enough to have so many windows that we are able to create a narrative running through them, whether that is very literal or whether it's abstract. It's also about developing a language to speak within the windows. The language could be a series of colours, shapes or textures. You do not have much time to grab the attention of the public; you need to grab them straight away while they pass, but at the same time there should be details that want to make the customers stay there longer if they want to. And of course, the windows need to be informative."

Alannah is also keen to enlist the help of artists and other noted creative individuals to design her windows. "One of our creative strategies is to collaborate with others, whether that means working with a fashion designer to create an exclusive window or bring in either unknown or famous artists to design a complete scheme," she explains. "I find they all bring such huge talent to the store. We understand how to work with them and also how to get the best from them. It's good to have an open mind and ask for other points of view."

**Above**
In its "Future Punk" windows, which some viewers might find slightly disturbing, Selfridges in London provocatively cross-fertilizes the subjects of sex and cookware.

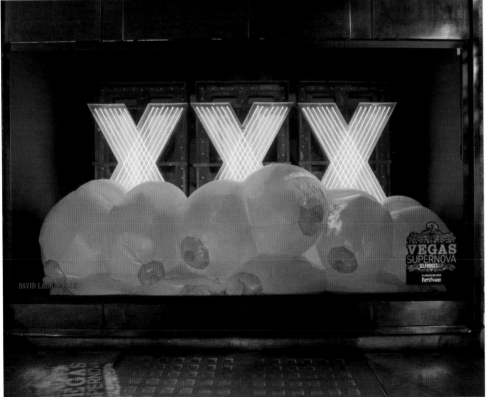

**Above and below**

Designed by David LaChapelle, inflatable breasts fill a Selfridges window in London to suggest the seedier side of Las Vegas for a month-long "Vegas Supernova" promotion. The theme aimed to offer an experience other than shopping and to attract a different kind of customer to the store. The dynamism of the display was heightened by the fact that as the breasts deflated, neon signs hidden behind were slowly revealed.

# Themes and schemes

**Both themes and schemes are familiar words to a visual merchandiser. They refer to the creative element that will be used to support the product. They are both related, giving the window or windows a thread that will pull the overall look together. A theme or scheme should be well planned and thought through. Visual merchandisers use them to create drama, to tell a story and to inspire. They can be seasonal or a commentary upon social, political or economic trends.**

A theme is the topic of the window presentation. It should include the colour, the props and the relevant merchandise that will make the overall idea come to life. A swimwear theme may include sand, palm trees and a blue wall, thus giving the feel of a beach. Even a store with one window should have a window theme.

Schemes suit stores with many windows, like department stores such as Macy's in New York or Selfridges in London. A scheme takes on the theme but may be adapted so that each window is different, yet tells the same message. A beach window may have another

positioned next to it with a yacht and a blue floor; the next may have a hotel balcony as its main feature. It is important that the scheme is cohesive and consistent.

In many instances, window themes and schemes will be carried into the store and used in the in-store displays as well. When used properly, such displays will project a stronger message to the customer. Print-work such as graphics or signage reflecting the window message is the most effective and economical way of carrying the themes in-store. In-store displays at designated areas within the store can also carry the window theme inside. It is always worth considering where to place the in-store displays to gain maximum exposure; extra mannequins or props can incur additional costs.

**Above**
The best way of viewing a window scheme is from across the street. Here at Harvey Nichols, London, large graphics, mannequins and props are used to create impact.

**Above**
Harvey Nichols, in its true
outlandish style, makes the most
of its tall windows by using every
available space to create an
innovative window scheme.

BRIGHT
YOUNG 2013
THINGS
selfridges.com/byt    #BYT2013

GRACE HAMILTON
ACCESSORIES
*Driven by a love of vintage, Grace's innovative designs are inspired by her travels to Tanzania and Zanzibar. Her accessories are hand-crafted using macramé, crochet and knitting techniques. grace.hamilton.co.uk*
*Visit her in the concept store on G.*

Multiple chain stores often invest time and money presenting their flagship store in an eye-catching way. Clearly because the flagship store is larger, the window scheme can be dramatic and create more impact. The challenge for the visual merchandising manager for a chain is to deliver the same message through the smaller stores as well. This can be done by using a common thread, such as a colour, a graphic or a prop. All the windows are likely to be different sizes, even within multiple chain stores, so often more than one option of display needs to be designed and produced.

Deciding on a window theme is not always easy. There may be a number of factors hindering creative licence. The budget immediately springs to mind, but more important may be the need to design around specific items of merchandise selected by the retailer. On many occasions, especially

with high-street stores, the merchandise you can use may have already been targeted for the windows, possibly due to its presence in a major advertising campaign. This will generally be the same for certain sale items that need to be cleared quickly from the store. In that instance, it is always best to start off with a simple yet effective design that will win the support of the retailer.

Understanding the products and the perceived image of the store will always be an advantage. More often than not, a store-owner enlisting the help of a professional visual merchandiser will expect the product to be presented well and to be the prominent feature within the window, with props used in a supporting role. If, however, you have more creative freedom to choose the product, you should first understand the theme and then consider what look and message you hope to project to the customers. For example,

**Above**
The "Bright Young Things" window scheme at Selfridges, London, showcases innovative new designers. This dramatic window promotes the work of the jewellery designer Grace Hamilton.

choosing a selection of traditional furniture and home accessories to go with a contemporary window theme may not work, as it will create a less direct statement. It is always wise to research the product and the window scheme beforehand. Fashion dressers should also look for key trends that can inspire the public. A 1960s fashion revival collection may sit better with furniture from the same era against a black-and-white backdrop than placed in an ethnic or rural setting. The product on most occasions will help dictate what the overall window presentation will look like. It is best to start by brainstorming ideas and ascertain what message you expect the customer to perceive from the presentation; rarely is the first idea put into action. One should also consider the style and shape of the products and what would support them.

When looking for an idea for a story or theme for your window, try to be imaginative and inspirational. Remember that trying to recreate a realistic setting will look forced and unnatural if the mannequin is not suited to a particular pose, such as holding a champagne glass or a dancing stance.

**Above and below**
Part of a range of windows from Topman, these windows show how a theme can be carried from the flagship store through to the smallest of outlets in the chain. In the window of the flagship store in London, a shed covered in red-and-white gingham dominates the window. Rather than taking the shed as a theme through to the smaller stores, gingham is chosen and adapted for use in another store with a back to its window.

### Colour

The use of colour offers an economical and a dramatic effect that can easily be changed to suit a window theme. There is no room for subtlety when choosing a colour for a window display. Strong, bold colours will make a difference, whereas an off-white instead of a pure white may not be noticeable from outside. Stripes, checks and fabric applications will help create theatre (see pages 84–89). By simply taking a colour from an individual piece of merchandise and replicating it on the wall of the window with paint, you will already have created a coordinated theme.

Metallic colours have a festive feel; they will also attract viewers at night time during longer winter nights, as they will reflect light from surrounding streetlamps and other lights.

### Sex, politics and social statements

These have often been used as window themes. Shocking a customer will undoubtedly get a reaction and, therefore, the attention of that customer, although sometimes not quite the reaction the retailer expects. Live models and pole dancers have been featured in Selfridges' windows. Alannah Weston insists that the theme is paramount in creating a successful window. "The theme is important because it tells the customer where you are in terms of what's going on in the world," she says. "A lot of our themes might come from the major fashion shows or even the art world, or they may come from what's going on culturally. That gives us a very strong direction, and then you build your language on top of that. My team are incredible because they come from different backgrounds: some are from art backgrounds, some from fashion – I even have someone who studied construction. They all have great ideas, and that is what makes our windows so contemporary."

**Above**
The use of a bold, dynamic blue on the back walls and on the mannequins provides a dramatic backdrop to these "Afro Chic" windows.

**Above**

Selfridges' "Vegas Supernova" window scheme in London, here featuring neon pole dancers, was inspired by the city's centenary and the Vegas-like glitz concurrently circulating in the fashion world. By adopting such a theme, Selfridges was able to create a window scheme that caused a buzz among the public.

## Christmas

For many retailers, Christmas is the time when the visual merchandising team excels with its window schemes and themes. Stores in most major cities compete for the best windows. Large budgets and huge amounts of time are spent preparing these festive extravaganzas. The months of November and December are prime selling times for retailers, and not to enter the competition would be short-sighted and naive.

**Above**
Specially commissioned, full-scale topiary trees are the main feature of this elaborate Christmas presentation at Selfridges, London.

**Below**
A traditional festive landscape acts as a backdrop in this Fortnum & Mason window in London. Subtle shades of blue and white help create a wintry window scheme that appeals to both young and old.

# Budgeting

**Retailers will expect big promotions to draw more attention than usual to the store. These will be costly, and it is essential to plan and budget for such events. An annual window budget should be divided to cover all the costs of the planned window schemes. Most retailers will mix expensive and overstated windows with more modestly priced schemes during the course of a year.**

A Christmas scheme will always incur the most cost. Any seasonal window run will need to be planned early; many prop-makers, freelance dressers and window technicians are in demand. It is always wise to ensure that any extra help required is budgeted for and booked in advance.

Multiples of the same object are a quick solution for a more economical window scheme.

**Above**
The sheer mass of bunting in this window in Urban Outfitters' London store creates a dramatic scene. The bust forms move the main prop (the bunting) with their articulated arms, and one has a camera with which to take pictures of the public.

# Props

Once you have chosen your theme and scheme and your merchandise, it is then time to consider the props you will need before thinking about the layout of the window itself. Props, as the name suggests, are objects that visually support the items for sale. A window display can include one prop or a whole collection. A prop can have empathy with the products, or cleverly have nothing in common with the merchandise at all. A padded silk box would be a conventional way to support a diamond ring; a roll of barbed wire would be a contemporary way of showing the same piece. One stand-alone prop can be as effective as a whole window scheme fashioned from many. Props enhance a window or an interior display, and they work in the same way as on film sets or a theatrical stage. They can be purchased or bespoke. Other merchandise items can also be used as props, such as a stock item of furniture used as a backdrop for a fashion scheme. Such props are both economical and commercial because one would not need to pay for them to be made; they can display a price ticket and can be sold themselves.

The general rule for props is that they should support the product without overpowering it: a basic mix of two-thirds props to one-third merchandise is usually best. This may seem an odd balance, but the props are there to support the theme and to provide drama, so they need to be bold enough to create an impression. Too much merchandise can interfere with the artistic composition – unless that is the intention, such as during a clearance sale, when the aim is to focus on the reduction message. Skilled visual merchandisers, however, will have the confidence to ignore this rule if preferable. There should always be interaction between the props and the product. A plant pot placed at the foot of a mannequin will draw attention for the wrong reasons; it will undoubtedly look out of place and have no relevance to the merchandise it is supporting. It is best to avoid props that are personal favourites if they have nothing in common with the window theme. Small boutiques with no visual guidance are often the worst offenders in this common habit; old pieces of furniture, drapes and artificial flowers unthoughtfully placed in a window with no relevance to the merchandise will look dull and out of place.

Many newcomers to the world of visual merchandising may be concerned about the cost of such items. Of course, a well-made prop may put the retailer on the same ladder as the major department stores. Some of the best windows, however, are crafted not with a heavy bank balance but with an active imagination. Bergdorf Goodman in New York, famous for its lavish window displays, once covered the entire back walls of its vast windows with burnt toast graded from light to dark, with stylishly dressed mannequins at the front. The windows would have cost no more than the price of some loaves of bread and a toaster – unlike the store's famed Christmas windows, on which huge amounts are spent.

There are a variety of ways to use and source props to achieve stunning window displays.

**Opposite**
Expensive and maybe not quite politically acceptable, but the use of a life-sized deer to display fashion accessories at Printemps in Paris is an example of the many exotic props that are available for hire.

### Props en masse

An interesting way to introduce props to a window is to arrange them en masse. Acquire something cheap and easily available, such as an empty tin can, for example. By itself on the floor next to an item of furniture, it may look lost and bear no obvious relation to the window theme. Used en masse, however – possibly covering the wall or floor – the cans become a bold statement, just as stacking hundreds of bottles of the same perfume aesthetically changes the emphasis from product to prop, but cleverly uses the merchandise to do this.

### Bespoke props

Handmade props will possibly incur some costs; however, they are generally worth the extravagance. If the visual merchandiser requires items made especially for a window scheme, he or she will either approach a prop-maker or make them personally. A professional prop-maker will take the brief away and develop the concept further; it is wise to see a sample to check for sizing/colour/finish before committing to the final design. Only when the client is happy with the designs will manufacture of the finished design begin. It is always wise to use prop-makers who have an understanding of window displays, as they will know when to cut corners on the overall finish yet consider the project as a whole and deliver a finished prop on time, to a high standard and within the budget agreed. Prop-makers will also be specialists in carpentry and paint finishes, and will also be able to work with many other materials. When briefing the prop-maker, it is worth remembering that a closed window will only require the prop to be finished on one side, as the back will not be seen from the street, but a prop for an open window will need to be finished on all sides so that it can be viewed from 360 degrees.

Build up a collection of generic props that can be reused and interchanged, or even carried into the store interior at a later date.

**Above**
These simple bust forms used en masse form a very powerful display, showing as it does the authority and range of a coat collection available in-store in Topshop, London. The simple slogan "COATS" also highlights the product.

**Below**
Arranged in a carefully constructed rectangle, these simple slate tiles displayed in a Macy's New York window create a subtle support for the mannequin, which is itself dressed in neutral clothing.

**Opposite**
The clever use of rope as a prop at Liberty's, London, is used to carefully suspend mannequins for a dramatic window scheme.

Fresh flowers are an effective way to promote a specific season.

### Recycling props

Resourceful visual merchandisers will store props and use them again at a later date, possibly in the windows once more, but with a new finish or – more often than not – in the interior of the store. One should try to get as much mileage out of the props as possible, especially if they were costly. However, they should not be overexposed; the customer will expect to see something new. Remember that well-manufactured props can be used in-store at another time. Many visual merchandisers will shrewdly pick up items from salvage shops and reuse them at a later date. It is worth remembering that large, overpowering props can only be used so often before the public begins to recognize them behind the makeovers. Smaller discreet items, on the other hand, can be painted and decorated in many ways and used in a multitude of displays if interchanged with other props.

### Flora

Flowers and plants can be very effective in a window presentation but may not live long; the heat from the sun and from the window lighting can wither even the healthiest of plants in just a few hours. Artificial plants have become much more realistic over the years, and can be cleaned, packed up, stored and used again.

### Evaluating props

Getting the most from the props one chooses will not only help complete the window display but will also make the job of a visual merchandiser a lot easier. It is always worth planning how and when to use props, as well as what they ultimately will contribute to a window display. A prop may have been costly and look good on paper, but always question whether it is truly effective.

**Above**
The use of these artificial flowers brings a fresh, spring-like theme to this Topshop window in London, with the advantage that they will not wilt or die.

**Opposite**
Artificial topiary has been used on a bust form at Fortnum & Mason, London, to display ladies' fashion jewellery.

# Designing a window display

**Having chosen the merchandise, the theme and the props, there are a few simple preparations a visual merchandiser needs to make to ensure that the window installation process goes smoothly.**

## Sketch

The first stage in designing a window is to sketch out a proposed layout. Professionals will make a rough plan of how they want the finished window to look. These rough drawings are often not to scale, but they reassure the designer that the overall completed window presentation will work. Many visual merchandisers who are required to present their window schemes to third parties may need a detailed diagram drawn to scale. These two-dimensional visuals are usually created with the help of a computer-aided design program (CAD). An experienced CAD user can produce a realistic suggestion of the window design. For beginners, a Photoshop program will suffice. Only the most experienced visual merchandisers can confidently enter a window and produce a work of art without a detailed diagram. The more hands-on experience gained, the less detailed the sketches will need to be. Tried-and-tested windows will always succeed.

**Above**
A simple, hand-drawn sketch that can then incorporate colour and texture will give you an idea of the overall look of your window design. This particular layout is an example of pyramid grouping (see page 78).

1 The merchandise is grouped together to reflect the form of a pyramid.

2 A large vase helps to anchor the pyramid on the left-hand side.

3 This vase sits at the top of the pyramid.

4 A table on the right-hand side of the display creates optical balance with the vase on the left-hand side.

5 The use of two colours in the display helps to create a more dramatic image.

6 Eye level, also the focal point, as the window would be viewed by a passer-by in the street, is slightly off-centre.

7 The display faces the street and is positioned in the centre of the window to gain maximum attention.

8 CAD allows experimentation with different textures in the design, here allowing selection of the best wallpaper.

**Above**
A CAD version can be made to scale and used as a more professional means of presenting your window-display ideas to colleagues.

**Below**
Erwan and Ronan Bouroullec design for the window of Issey Miyake's Apoc store in Paris shows how CAD can be used to organize products in a window.

## Layout

There are a series of rules and standards that the visual merchandiser should consider when laying out a window. However, like many professionals who rely on guidelines, experienced visual merchandisers often break them, either because they wish to be controversial or because they have the skill to know exactly how and when to leave tradition behind. Before novices take on more than they can chew, however, it is always wise to understand the basic rules. Once this valuable knowledge is instilled in them, they will have a deeper understanding of the ethics behind designing a window and of how best to capture the public's attention.

## Focal point

Large or small, a window needs to have a focal point on which, when viewed from the street, the eye will instinctively rest. Larger windows may need more than one. The focal point is best placed just below eye level, just off-centre. The eye may then be guided around the window display to other products. Remember: if a window is higher than the pavement, the focal point will have to be lower. It is always best to view the window from outside to ascertain where the main focus should be. Customer flow will also affect the way the window is viewed. If the majority of pedestrians approach the window from the left, then the grouping should be aimed to the left; it would be a shame to spend valuable time planning and dressing a window only for the bulk of customers to notice the back of the mannequins, merchandise or props.

**Above**
A typical pyramid grouping that can be used for both homeware and fashion. The focal point is the dark red vase on the second shelf of the unit at the back, just off-centre. It is important to make the focal point eye-catching.

It is unwise to position the main products or props on the side walls, leaving a large void in the centre of the window, just as it is foolish to hang key items too high in the window, as the eye may be guided to the ceiling and thus out of the window.

Deep windows can be problematic. The visual merchandiser often positions product groupings towards the front of the glass, hoping that they will get the maximum exposure from the display. However, by placing some items at the front with more behind leading back to the wall, a customer's eye can be encouraged to follow the carefully positioned objects back into the window. This also applies to centre displays with product trailing out towards the side walls.

Optical balance

Understanding the term "balance" when designing and installing a window display is essential. To a visual merchandiser, the composition of the window display relates to how the product is aesthetically balanced. Correct balance is achieved when the presentation shares equal optical weight. There are two main compositions: informal balance, known as asymmetrical, and formal balance, known as symmetrical. Both can be effective if executed correctly. Formal balance is easier to comprehend because the same objects are used to create a mirror image. Informal balance relies on the visual merchandiser using various objects but still creating an even distribution of the optical weight.

Using odd numbers is also a general rule when grouping products or mannequins. Three mannequins positioned tightly together will appear stronger than two.

**Above**
The first group in the illustration (top) shows two identical vases, which clearly balance. The second group (bottom), however, shows products that are different on each side of the shelf, but optically their weight is the same and so they also balance.

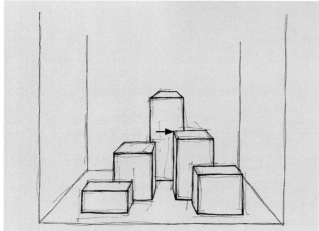
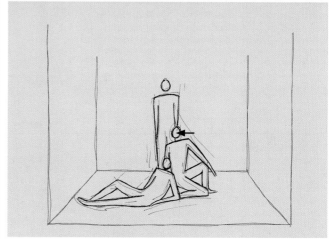

## Groupings

Arranging products in an aesthetic way is referred to as "grouping". There are two styles of grouping commonly used: pyramid and repetition groupings.

### Pyramid grouping

Any noted visual merchandiser who has been trained in the art of window display will be aware of "pyramid" grouping. For years, both in-store and in windows, this common rule has been practised around the world. The idea is that both props and products create pyramids. Aesthetically, it is a proven way to group products together so that the eye focuses on one main point first and is then led on to other focal points around it. The pyramid also enables the eye to remain for longer on the key product that is being emphasized.

**Above**
This window at Selfridges, London, was designed by pop group Empire of the Sun. The striking mannequin strokes two lions positioned on a lower level than him, creating a pyramid.

**Below left**
In this pyramid grouping, the focal point is at the left-hand side of the second-largest box.

**Below right**
In the pyramid grouping, the focal point in this group of mannequins is the head of the central figure.

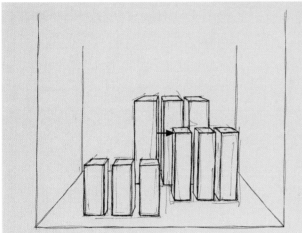

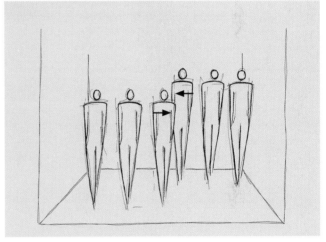

## Repetition grouping

Repetition grouping is another interesting way of arranging products. This style of dressing sounds straightforward and simple; however, only the most talented of visual merchandisers can produce outstanding repetition groupings. It is easy to lose the focal point within a window with repetition; never assume that the centre prop will be the focal point if it does not stand out enough to gain attention. A line of three mannequins may not have an obvious focal point, so sometimes you might have to work hard to create the focal point using merchandise; thus, the jacket on the centre mannequin could be brighter or bolder and be used to navigate your eye into the window. Placing the bold jacket on the end run of five mannequins may lead your eye to the side of the window and out. The aim is to use multiples of the same products to create a stronger presentation. Three perfume bottles will have more authority than one; 30 will undoubtedly have more impact.

On occasion, repetition groupings can be built up to create pyramids. Pyramid and repetition groupings generally do not work well together; the overall effect can look messy, with no main focus or design aesthetic.

**Above**
Three male mannequins stand rigidly together to create a strong repetition grouping in this French Connection window in London.

**Below left**
It is harder to find the focal point in a repetition grouping. The different heights employed in this window by the three staggered blocks means that it naturally falls off-centre on the left-hand side of the medium-sized blocks.

**Below right**
In this window, six mannequins are split into two groups, with three at the back and three at the front. Depending on whether you stand on the left or the right of the window, the focal point could change. From the left, it will fall on the third mannequin from the left in the front row; this is because the second row will be hidden behind the first. From the right, the focal point would be on the third mannequin in from the right in the back row. Both focal points need to be planned when dressing the window.

# Store study:
# Au Printemps

Au Printemps has been a pillar of the Parisian shopping culture since 1865, when Jules Jaluzot created the world-famous store that is still an important part of the Right Bank's architectural heritage. The word *printemps* means "springtime". Today, the once-exclusive French store has a presence in cities ranging from Tokyo to Jeddah. Its window displays are appreciated around the world for their quirky concepts and attention to detail, but its innovative ideas remain true to the original French brand that still makes Au Printemps a world-renowned destination store.

Franck Banchet, Au Printemps' Creative Director, graduated from the CTE, a private school specializing in visual merchandising. After this excellent training he went on to manage the fashion floors at Au Printemps' rival, Le Bon Marché, eventually moving to Au Printemps. Today, after ten years at Au Printemps, he instigates the creative concepts not only for the windows but also the vast interiors of 17 department stores.

### Which of the windows that you have designed is your favourite?

"To visualize a window is to offer an interpretation, a vision of a certain world or a theme. I love working with artists or designers to construct a story together. Our visions blend and we produce something very strong. One of the installations that made an impression on me were the windows we created with Bettina Rheims, because of their minimalist aspect and, overall, for the unique opportunity I had to meet and work with the "Queen" of photography.

Also, the living window with the choreographer Joëlle Bouvier, for the emotion it brought to the customers; people were stopping in their tracks to watch the live installation evolve.

Another favourite is the Christmas scheme that we devised with Karl Lagerfeld for Chanel. I like his creative, dreamlike worlds and his attention to detail. He created a dummy Mademoiselle Coco especially for Au Printemps that we placed in the *animées* (animated) windows of Boulevard Haussmann. This was an unbelievable experience, and the result of combining Mademoiselle Coco with our Christmas theme was magical."

### What is the hardest product category for which to design a window scheme?

"All product categories are a creative challenge, as far as window displays are concerned. But having to design a window scheme for jewellery, watches or even cosmetics, in 6-meter-wide windows is often the most difficult."

**Above**
A window to promote the late British designer Alexander McQueen: a strikingly posed mannequin seated on a sculpted bow is all that is needed.

### How do you start to plan and design a window scheme?

"The first step is to define a theme and concept for the window. Then, you have to find 'THE' idea; that very special idea that will make the difference."

### Is good lighting both in-store and in windows key?

"Good lighting is essential. It's the base for a good window display and it's totally part of the whole design. A window that is not lit properly will not have the same visual impact. It is essential to illuminate the whole window with an ambient light, and then use lights with a smaller beam width to highlight certain focal points, such as the mannequin's face. But the lighting can equally be a dynamic visual element in itself. Techniques such as the use of neon can illustrate a theme and illustrate the concept behind the window display."

### You produce amazing windows with great colour schemes. How important is the use of colour when designing a window scheme?

"Just like the use of lighting, colour is an element that can highlight a theme or a product. But colour can encourage mental associations, such as white for purity. I love playing with these preconceptions and 'upsetting' these codes in order to better serve the general theme of the display."

### Do you consider the merchandise before you design the window or do you make the product fit into the window scheme?

"In reality the merchandising and the windows form a unity. Our role is to enhance the value of a product and also to consider the development of the general concept. We then apply this concept in the display. One of the best examples is the way we realized the theme Operation Alice in Wonderland of Au Printemps (*l'Opération Alice au Printemps des Merveilles*). To coincide with Tim Burton's film *Alice in Wonderland*, we asked designers such as Maison Martin Margiela, Alexander McQueen and Christopher Kane to recreate Alice's dress. We then presented these designs, drawing inspiration from the world of Burton's film. And we did so in both the display and the merchandising."

**Above**
This window showcases a collaboration between Au Printemps and the launch of the film *Alice in Wonderland*. The quirky mannequin has been styled with a rabbit's head and wears a designer dress.

### What has been the most challenging window to design and install?

"Every year, we are challenged to produce exceptional Christmas windows. We have to plan in advance, be innovative and reinvent ourselves while respecting the traditions associated with this seasonal festivity. We also know that our Christmas windows are expected to surprise the public. The whole of Paris looks forward to the unveiling of the completed window scheme; we want the windows to be dreamlike, and appeal to both adults and children. In many of the windows we use animation, which is always challenging to plan and install but rewarding when you see the final outcome."

### Where does your creative inspiration come from?

I think I am inspired by all things in life: the street, travel, exhibitions, even video clips, photography ... although to be honest, I do not realize this when I capture a trend; I am just lucky to have the ability to catch the spirit of the times."

### Whose window displays do you admire?

"Barneys' and Liberty's windows are always the pinnacle of the avant-garde: original and highly creative."

### How important is store design? Does it help sell products?

"Definitely. Window displays act like an advert in the media: they are the "branding signature" of the store and, as such, the most direct advertising message. The product is part of a whole scenography, but the windows help enforce the store's overall creativity, the key element that encourages the public to step into the store and spend."

**Above**
This clever window scheme consisted of various forms of transport carrying bundles wrapped in exquisite fabrics, all colour coordinated.

### How important are signage and graphics both in-store and in windows?

"A company's brand identity is reflected through the use of graphics and signage. It contributes to its brand positioning, but has to be sympathetic with the artistic style and must sit comfortably with the overall brand. This is all the more true for Au Printemps, as we have 17 stores in France. So we have to ensure that our customers identify with the personality of our signage, whether they are in Paris, Lyon or Marseilles."

### What will store windows be like in 50 years' time?

"Interactive windows: that is to say, windows without glass."

### Whose mannequins do you like to work with most?

"Adel Rootstein's. They have great proportions and beautiful postures."

**Above**
A dramatic mannequin is reflected by cleverly positioned mirrors. Hoops of neon highlight the model and add a theatrical quality.

# Colour

**The use of colour can create drama and atmosphere. Most retailers rely on colour as an inexpensive tool to change the window's look and image. Colour can be added in many ways, the most obvious being paint. Lighting, fabric and graphics can also create impact.**

Colours can be extremely personal; not everyone's tastes and preferences are the same. In different cultures, colours may mean different things. For example, pink is seen as the navy blue of India. Some colours have an almost global reference. Red is seen by many as a warning colour, known to get one's heart racing; this is possibly why it is also the colour used by most retailers at sale times, when they encourage a shopping frenzy by ensuring their customers literally "see red". The mint-green aprons that British surgeons wear are by no means a fashion statement; they are in fact coloured that way because the eye will settle more easily looking at them after focusing on the colour of blood – light green is calming. Many mental-health institutions colour their walls with the same shade. With this in mind, it is worth considering the impact that colour can have on a customer looking at a window display.

Using the wrong colours can, of course, be detrimental to a retailer. The autumn/winter 2006 fashion collections, into which the British high street bought heavily, struggled to sell because of their colour: grey. Many women especially felt that the colour was drab and hard to wear without looking dull. The visual merchandiser could have tackled this problem by complementing it with accessories, backdrop colours or an imaginative display.

It is useful for visual merchandisers to understand the basic principles of colour and what effects different colours may have on their customers. The colour wheel is certainly the most effective way of understanding how colours work.

**Above**
A collaboration between the luxury French fashion house Louis Vuitton and the Japanese artist Yayoi Kusama was skilfully created for Selfridges, London, using a sophisticated colour scheme of just red and white with highlights of metallic gold.

Primary ▬▬▬

Secondary ▬▬▬

Tertiary — —

## The colour wheel

In the late seventeenth and early eighteenth centuries, Sir Isaac Newton created the very first colour wheel. By use of a prism, he split sunlight into colours to create a colour spectrum. A century later, the German writer Johann Wolfgang von Goethe produced his own version of a colour wheel based on the psychological effect of colours, where reds and oranges were positive and greens to blues more unsettling.

The colour wheel that is used today is based on three primary colours: yellow, red and blue. When mixed together, these three colours produce every other colour. By blending two of the primary colours, a secondary colour is created: yellow and red mixed together will make orange, for instance. A primary colour mixed with a secondary colour will form a tertiary colour: yellow and green, for example, create yellow-green.

## Colour terms

Chromatic

High colour density: red, blue and yellow.

Achromatic

The opposite of chromatic: grey, white and black.

Shade

Adding black to a colour will alter the appearance of the colour and make it darker: a different shade of the original colour.

Tint

Adding white to a colour will brighten the colour, creating different tints of the original colour.

Hue

Another name for the pure colour: red, blue, etc.

Value

The darkness or lightness of a colour.

**Above**
The 12 colours of this colour wheel consist of the three primaries, the secondary colours and the tertiary colours.

By painting the walls and floor in different colours, each will stand out to frame the product. It is also the perfect way to create a realistic room set.

### Colour schemes

To a novice visual merchandiser, exploring the use of colour and determining what effects it can have in a display may at first be daunting. Coordinating colours so that they are effective should be considered thoroughly before designing or installing a display. The most common colour schemes are based on just six variations (see opposite).

One of the most effective window schemes that has been used by visual merchandisers worldwide is the use of only one colour. Various shades of the same colour used in the same display can create impact. A window based on the colour blue, for example, can add an emotional value; it could be perceived as cold, sad or – depending on the hue – warm. By using the relatively inexpensive medium of paint on the walls in one shade of blue and adding mannequins in another shade and the product in different shades

again, the window will look striking and will be cost-effective, too. Depending on the dressing and styling, colour can also promote a trend: pink for Valentine's Day, for example; red for Christmas; black for a luxury fashion look.

**Above**
A monochromatic window can be very effective and easy to design. Here at Selfridges, London, a solid black floor and chequered wall help complement the contemporary furniture display in collaboration with *Elle Decoration.*

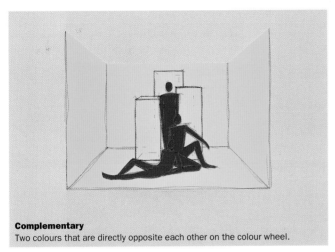

**Complementary**
Two colours that are directly opposite each other on the colour wheel.

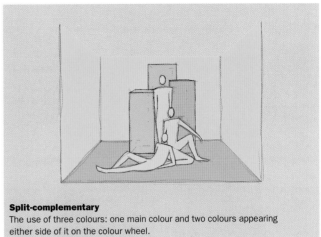

**Split-complementary**
The use of three colours: one main colour and two colours appearing either side of it on the colour wheel.

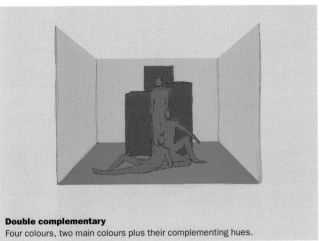

**Double complementary**
Four colours, two main colours plus their complementing hues.

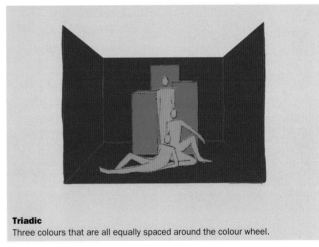

**Triadic**
Three colours that are all equally spaced around the colour wheel.

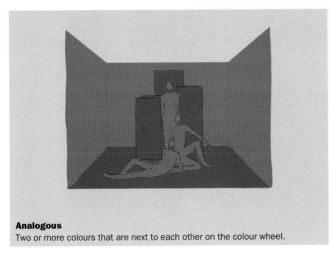

**Analogous**
Two or more colours that are next to each other on the colour wheel.

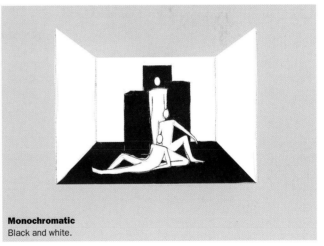

**Monochromatic**
Black and white.

**Above**
The use of colour in a window display is paramount in its success. These examples demonstrate how colour can be used as a tool for attracting the customer's attention.

Colour really is the most magnificent tool for capturing the attention of passers-by and creating atmosphere. If in doubt, always go for the brighter or darker option. Taking the soft option will not be as effective and will be perceived as predictable by the customer who may overlook the colour scheme – cream instead of crisp white will appear weak, and the wrong shade of red may look like a sale window.

When using colour, it also pays to consider the colour associations behind the product itself. Whereas a window promoting eco-friendly products would benefit from the window being coloured in neutral tones associated with natural products – ecru, cream and off-white – a butcher would never use red as a backdrop for produce; instead he uses white because it will always appear hygienic and show off the cuts of meat. A jeweller specializing in diamonds will, of course, rely on a rich, dark colour that will offset the gems and make them sparkle.

There are also tricks you can use with colour to change the look of the window. A darker colour such as black will make a large window appear smaller. White, on the other hand, will create the effect of space. Painting or applying vertical stripes to the window walls will visually stretch it.

**Opposite**
The mask in this window from Printemps in Paris appears to be floating against the black background, giving the complete window a real sense of drama. Painting a large window black will make it appear smaller and also create great atmosphere.

**Above**
Painting stripes on a wall will make the window appear taller as well as create an interesting and economical wall treatment, seen here for the "Spring Beauty" display at Selfridges in London.

**Below**
A neutral window scheme made entirely from light wood set against a white backdrop is brought to life with just one desirable Céline handbag in red at Selfridges, London.

# Window prepping

**Once it has been decided which products are to be used, it is wise to collect everything and prepare it beforehand. This will save valuable dressing time.**

Preparing merchandise, or "prepping" as it is commonly known, will speed up the window-dressing process. Clothing can be selected in advance and ironed or steamed, price tags can be removed, and in some cases, mannequins can be dressed away from the windows and added later. Fashion dressers may often require hosiery and other accessories; these should also be selected during the prep time.

Household goods can be picked and prepped: glasses cleaned, labels removed and fabrics ironed. The more prepping that is done in advance, the less work there will be when a window is being dressed. Once the products are selected and prepped, they can be added to the window.

**Above**
An impressive window display at Fortnum & Mason, London. The complete structure on which the product has been placed rotates. Any movement within a window will attract customers' attention, because they are used to viewing static displays.

**Above**
A life-size and realistic giraffe fills
an entire window at Louis Vuitton,
London. This window has been
designed not only to display products
but also to attract customers through
its quirkiness.

# Installing the window display

**No retailer wants shop windows to be either empty or in a state of undress for long. It is therefore important that a feasible time slot is allocated to dress a window from start to finish. Unless the window scheme is complicated and needs to be dressed over a couple of days, a visual merchandiser should ensure that the window is completed in a day. Many visual merchandisers start early in the morning in order to strip out the existing window scheme while the store is closed so as not to hinder the customers by trailing props and products across the shop floor. It is also an easier time to bring the new scheme to the window.**

If the window scheme has been planned accurately, the subsequent dressing of the window should be trouble-free. It is essential that the window about to be dressed is clean and tidy; checks should be made to ensure all the lighting is working and that lightbulbs have not blown. It is easier to erect a step-ladder and replace lightbulbs before the window is full. Staples, nails and screws from

the previous dressing will need to be removed and, in many cases, holes in walls will need to be filled and sanded down.

Next, the walls should be treated. The floor should be left for last in order to avoid unnecessary paint splashes. If the walls are to be painted, it is often wise to start very early in the day, as they may require several coats and, depending on the weather, they may take a long time to dry. Leaving the lighting on will also help raise the temperature by a few degrees. It is advisable to mask off the edges of the glass close to the walls; paint-speckled glass will be noticeable to the customer. If the window has a solid floor such as marble or wood, this should also be covered to prevent paint splashes unless it, too, is being painted.

If the window has floorboards cut from MDF, they can be removed and covered away from the window while the walls are being painted, thus saving time. Covering large boards with either fabric or PVC can be difficult purely because of their size – assistance may be needed. As part of your toolbox (see page 217) a staple gun and a pair of scissors are a

**Above**
The façade of Liberty in London is impressive, but it also demands that the customer focuses a little more on what is for sale in the windows. Planning a window scheme that can compete with the architecture is important.

visual merchandiser's saviours; they will be required on many occasions, especially when covering panels. Always cut the fabric larger than the board, leaving enough spare to hold and pull while you staple. Start on the longest side first, putting a few staples in the middle of the board on both sides. Then do the same on the shorter sides, pulling the fabric taut; work towards each of the corners, securing the fabric with staples as you go. When you reach the corners, fold the fabric neatly under the board and add some final staples. Remember: you may also need to strip the boards for the next window scheme, so try to use as few staples as possible. Removing staples can be time-consuming and arduous.

With the walls painted and the floors finished, the dressing can commence. It is always advisable to introduce the props first – they will be the backbone of the whole window scheme. Position the props where you think they will attract attention, remembering that the products should be king and that the props must interact with the merchandise. Larger props are generally placed towards the back of the window, with smaller ones towards the front. It would be pointless to hide the products (and any other props) with a bulky prop. Any hanging props should be suspended first; they must be securely wired or fixed to the ceiling grid. Free-standing props can then be added and arranged.

Remember, mannequins are also props designed to support clothing. It is always worth considering where they will be positioned and how they will interact with the window scheme.

If the window is backless, the unappealing rear of a piece of furniture such as a cabinet will be in full view. Placing another cabinet backing onto it can hide the ugly side and can also be dressed to face in-store, giving the customer two chances to see the display: when entering and when leaving.

As with props, large products should be placed in the window first. It is important at this time to distribute the larger items so that they form the backbone of the main bulk of a grouping. A window may have many groupings, all trailing from one main grouping. The largest and main grouping should be made up of the largest item. A fridge-freezer, for example, could stand just off-centre, with a

**Above**
Subtle lighting and elegantly posed mannequins in the windows either side of the entrance to Saks Fifth Avenue, New York, help guide customers into the store.

**The 12 Dancing Princesses**

grouping of other electrical products around it; a washing machine may be positioned to the left, near but not touching the fridge-freezer with another selection of electrical items; to the right of the window a microwave could be positioned with a smaller group of electrical accessories. It is important that the largest grouping is installed first, before the smaller ones. Concentrating on one small area of the window before finishing the bigger area is not advisable, because it is the fully completed window as a whole that should be considered as the sales device, not just one specific area.

Checking the window from street level is essential. Spending long hours dressing a window without looking at it from the customer's viewpoint can lead to problems: the focal point might not be in the correct place and the whole window scheme may need to be adjusted, thus wasting time.

Closed windows can be claustrophobic and sometimes get very hot. It is always best, not only for one's sanity but also for creativity, to take breaks from difficult dressings. A five-minute rest may inspire and initiate ideas.

When a window is 90 per cent complete, it is time to adjust the lighting. The lighting is one of the most vital elements of a window display and, sadly, one that many visual merchandisers forget to adjust. Hours can

be spent dressing and perfecting a window display, so it makes sense to illuminate it to make it stand out to passers-by. A spotlight focused on an empty back wall can be very distracting – and at night, very visible.

Attention should be focused on the price tickets, if used; make sure that they are spelt correctly and that they are positioned adjacent to the relevant products. It is also important to make sure that the text used is large enough to be seen from the street. Finally, all surfaces should be cleaned and floors should be swept.

Some stores have the luxury of having a mock window in the studio, complete with lighting rig, where a whole window can be installed and dressed to see if the design works aesthetically. Multi-chain retailers might use this as a visual tool, once photographed, for visual guidelines that can then be sent out to regional stores.

**Above**
Illuminated skirts resemble lampshades in this Selfridges window in London. The window was designed to promote the launch of the store's women's shoe gallery, the largest shoe department in the world.

**Above**
A dramatic window scheme in Topshop, London. At first glance, it seems that the mannequins are simply grouped together to show off the latest trends, but after further scrutiny, it becomes apparent that the entire room they occupy is upside down.

# Store study:
# Louis Vuitton

Being the Creative Director for the most recognized luxury brand in the world could be stressful. Faye Mcleod takes it all in her stride and enjoys the challenge of designing and installing innovative window displays across the world. Originally from Scotland, Mcleod has worked in London, New York and now Paris for brands including Selfridges, Topshop, Liberty and Jigsaw. Now as the creative force behind the inspirational window displays for the French brand Louis Vuitton, she resides in Paris and works from an office on Pont Neuf. She and her team are responsible for the innovative window displays that show-case the season's "must-have" items that every fashionista desires.

**Louis Vuitton is recognized worldwide as a luxury brand. Does this have an impact on how the windows should look?**

"Definitely. The windows are always enticing and exciting, incorporating each with an element of surprise with the Louis Vuitton luxury consistent throughout."

**What techniques and practices do you have to consider that a high-street store would not?**

"As we work on each scheme we are able to experiment with the ideas, which includes prototyping everything in advance, giving us time to refine all the creative elements before the windows go 'live'. One example is the New Bond Street Maison: the 'Cabinets of Curiosity' window went through a number of different colour treatments of gold until we were able to arrive at the one we felt worked."

**How do you maintain the high standards set by Louis Vuitton across the globe?**

"All the creative ideas and decisions are made

**Above**
Metallic red balloons appear to be lifting a mannequin sat on a piece of iconic Louis Vuitton luggage in the windows of the Champs-Élysées store, Paris.

**Below**
A grey velvet quilted backdrop with gold pegs has been designed to hold the season's "must-have" handbags in the Louis Vuitton Maison flagship store in London.

in Paris, as this enables consistency and considered development for the brand. We communicate to all our teams around the globe on a regular basis, which allows the creative work to be executed carefully and accurately."

### Do you have teams of visual merchandisers working in each country? How do you communicate your creative concepts to them?

"We have visual-merchandising teams all over the world. To maintain consistency we produce detailed creative guidelines and technical booklets. We also put a lot of energy into communication – there are several global seminars that we all attend each year."

### Your windows often differ between countries and cities. Why is this?

"Windows can occasionally be tailored specifically to a location or event (New Bond Street, for example). We also work a great deal with artists, and these collaborations are often place-specific – for example Vik Muniz in Brazil and Stephen Sprouse in the USA."

### Where do you get your creative energy?

"Travel, my team, exhibitions, friends and yoga."

### You have collaborated with artists, stylists and influential fashionistas. How important is it to enlist the ideas of others?

"It's richly rewarding to work with other creative talents; this can push boundaries and inject a different approach to the studio. This was apparent when we recently collaborated with Katie Grand for the Louis Vuitton 'Ready to Wear' exhibition in the London Maison."

### You were recently in India. Did you get any inspiration for your future window schemes?

"Who knows? I did get to ride a painted elephant and returned to Paris neon pink thanks to the Holi festival of colour."

### Your Bond Street Maison store opens soon. What can the Louis Vuitton following expect?

"Hopefully something unexpected."

### Whose windows do you admire?

"Coco Maya (London), Ted Muehling (New York), Hermès (specifically Rue de Saint Honoré). Moschino, Marc Jacobs and Lanvin are always strong. Bergdorf Goodman is always elegantly 'luxury'."

### You started your career at Selfridges, London and have worked in New York, and now Paris. What's next?

"I'm happy where I am."

**Above**
Gold cotton-reels hold thread in a variety of colours in this eye-catching window scheme in the Louis Vuitton store on the Champs-Élysées, Paris.

**Below left to right**
White doves escape from their gilt cages and circle around a human head wearing Louis Vuitton glasses in Paris. The Eiffel Tower has arrived in New York at the Louis Vuitton store. This clever use of a vinyl decal has been applied to the exterior of the store, creating an arresting result.

# Lighting

**Paul Symes, the visual merchandising manager for London's Fortnum & Mason, has always had an obsessive interest in lighting and technical wizardry. His tips for ensuring a window is well lit are:**

Ensure all lamp fittings are cleaned and working before dressing a window.

While adjusting lighting, a simple way to see if the beam is focused on the correct product is to wave your hand in front of the lamp and see where the shadow falls.

Use lamps of the correct beam widths.

Have a supply of spare lamps at hand.

Check the window lighting during the day and at night.

Be certain that the light beams are aimed into the windows – not facing out towards the public, thus blinding potential customers.

**Lighting should never be an afterthought. The process of lighting a window should be planned at the same time as the window scheme (see the Lighting chart on page 219 for assistance).**

A track system with adjustable lamps offers the most flexibility in windows and gives the visual merchandiser the opportunity to use several different lamp fittings, each of which will perform a different role within the display. Spot fittings will highlight an individual piece of merchandise or mannequin, while flood fittings will give an ambient light to the whole.

The wattage and beam width of a lamp can be baffling to a novice. The actual lamp fitting is useless without the correct lamp. Many lighting fixtures can house a variety of lamps, but not all of them will be universally effective. The size of the beam width you require usually depends on the size of the grouping it is expected to highlight. A small piece of jewellery, for example, will only require a three-degree beam width; anything wider will illuminate the surrounding area. Large, deep windows may require flooding with a general wash of light before spotlights are used to highlight individual items. A run of windows should each have a similar quantity of light; a dark window placed in a run of ten will stand out for the wrong reasons, as will a very bright window.

Colour and the time of day also need to be taken into account when choosing lighting. Some colours absorb light and others will reflect it. If a light-absorbing colour such as black or dark blue is being used, extra lighting may be required to compensate. Fabrics and carpet will also absorb a substantial amount of the lighting in a window.

Lighting used in the daytime can differ from the amount needed at night. In a bright window with the sun shining on it, more light will be required to compensate for the extra daylight. Less lighting, as strange as it may seem, is required at night because the windows will stand out against their dark surroundings – there is little other lighting to compete with. Many retailers have adopted a lighting system that can automatically adjust the lighting outputs, depending on the time of the day.

**Above**
A detail from a scheme in Harvey Nichols shows how a narrow-beam pin spotlight can be used to highlight the mannequins, and how effective it can be carefully to coordinate the make-up with the theme.

**Opposite**
Theatrical lighting has been used to highlight the dramatic poses of these Adel Rootstein mannequins at the company's showroom in New York, enabling visual merchandisers to imagine how effective they might look in their own windows.

# Signage and graphics

There is no doubt that an illustration (graphic) or piece of text (signage) in a window is a sure-fire way to get a statement across to customers, be it price-driven or informative. Many visual merchandisers not only use graphics to tell a message but also as part of their window schemes. The use of bold, colourful text can enhance many window displays. Often, signage and graphics may be used as a statement to support the window theme, or sometimes as the prop that ties a window scheme together.

## Signage

It is worth noting that too much information can be confusing and text should be used cautiously. It is rather arrogant to expect shoppers to read reams of text in a window. It is always best to keep any text simple and explanatory; punchy one-liners always work best. Window signage should be planned at the same time as the scheme or theme – it should never be an afterthought. Always consider how the signage interacts with the window scheme or products, and question whether the text enhances the window or if it is unnecessary. Any signage used in a window should always be prioritized in order of importance. A ticket showing the price of an item of furniture may be more important to its sale than a sign stating its location in-store, while a banner offering a discount may overrule both. Either way, too many tickets, signs or graphics can lead to visual overkill.

The positioning of signage and the choice of colour must be thoroughly planned before-hand. A green message carefully placed on the glass will not stand out against a green back wall; a contrasting colour would work better. The same sign placed directly in front of the main grouping can either hide it or, if positioned correctly, draw the eye to it. Many retailers still place signage far too high in a window and expect the public to look up to read it. Positioning signage high in a window encourages the viewer's eye to leave the main focus of the window and trail off to the ceiling grid instead. The most common and conventional place for signage is at eye level from the street.

Graffiti, neon, TV monitors and projected images may all be used to send messages to the public, and the same general rules apply. To get the message across, text must be clear and easy to read and digest.

**Above**
Part of a sequence of windows entitled "Spring Beauty" at Selfridges, London. The text is the theme that runs through each window, each caption relating to a recognizable quotation or colloquialism.

**Above**
Large-scale text is applied to the windows here to create not only a larger window scheme called "Shop Like a Man", but also to interact with the T-shirts on display.

**Below**
A colourful window in Topshop, Westfield, London. Giant pansies decorate the two-storey façade of the store. The large plinth in coordinating colours with neon trim elevates the mannequins.

### Window signage

Window signage has progressed considerably over recent years. The once handwritten signs hanging from ceiling grids have been replaced with vinyl machine-cut letters that are usually stuck to the window glass. These state-of-the-art letters are accurately cut to a predetermined design by machine and can be produced in any colour or typeface. Applying the text to a window, unfortunately, still has to be done by hand. There are many companies that will not only cut the signage for you but also apply it. The task itself is not difficult; however, patience will be required. One small slip and the lettering can fold back on itself and become ruined. The vinyl letters can be positioned on the outside of the window or inside. Both are suitable, although bored customers have been known to pick the letters off the outside of the glass.

To apply the letters, a piece of masking tape is placed on the non-sticky side of the text. This holds the text in its correct format and makes the whole line or word easier to handle. Before placing the text onto the glass, many professionals will spray the glass with a weak soapy liquid; the vinyl lettering is then placed on the glass and the soapy water allows the lettering to be adjusted. When the text is positioned in the correct place, a plastic squeegee the size of a credit card is used to press down the letters and force the water from between the adhesive and the window glass. Finally, the masking tape is carefully pealed off, leaving the text firmly stuck to the glass. When the text is no longer required, it can simply be scraped away with a sharp blade.

The same vinyl treatment can be applied to the entire glass, thus blocking off the window completely. As strange as it may seem that a book teaching the art of window dressing should encourage such an idea, there may be times when a retailer needs to spend days, not hours, re-dressing a window. Many large department stores will use this opportunity to maximize the value of their window space and inform the public of the new window scheme or promotion at the same time. The windows act as a temporary billboard and hide the disarray inside.

**Above**
The impressive backdrop of this window display in Topshop, London, is constructed of steel. The letters have been cut out so that they appear rough and industrial-looking. Backlighting helps the text stand out.

## Descriptive tickets

Descriptive tickets are the signage used to inform the customer of prices, location of products or discounts. While many retailers prefer to be discreet and not inform the shopper of the price of an item, others proudly list the prices adjacent to the merchandise. When pricing the clothing on a mannequin, the ticket should always read from top to bottom, listing the prices starting from the top as the mannequin is dressed: i.e. hat, shirt, trousers, shoes. The lettering should be large enough to be seen from outside the window and be positioned to the right of the manne-quin. Each descriptive price ticket in the window should be the same size and format. Some retailers use a Perspex stand to hold the ticket, which can be purchased from display companies. Because of the static electricity in Perspex, however, such stands can act as a dust magnet and will need to be cleaned daily.

Merchandise can be priced in other ways, too. Smaller price tags may be pinned to clothing items, or household goods may have small tickets placed in among the groupings. Some items may need a description of the item to help the sale. An antique chair may require a brief history and list of the materials used in its construction; however, an edited version will suit most customers.

Handwritten tickets are definitely frowned upon in the visual merchandiser's world; even the smartest handwriting will look unprofessional. A printed ticket will always look better and be easier to read.

LO GO ™

Hat: £70

Jacket: £250

Knitwear: £150

Shirt: £124

Jeans: £110

Shoes: £190

### Graphics

Photography, either displayed within or applied to the window itself, is now a common tool for the visual merchandiser. Modern digital technology has made large-scale photographic prints affordable and accessible. As well as being used in conjunction with the retailer's advertising campaign, images are often created specifically for a window scheme. Such graphics have the advantage of being easy to install – and, as they don't have to be stored, easily thrown away. Photographic images can be applied to heavy-duty paper or card and hung from the lighting grid, printed on vinyl and applied to the window or printed on paper and stuck on the back wall. They can create an immediate window scheme that needs little advance planning and is quick to install. More than one skilled person will be needed to apply large-scale vinyl graphics to the glass. Care should be used in positioning them in the window. Ideally, they should not be applied to the side walls as they will only be seen by customers passing the window in one direction. Positioned on the back wall, however, they can be used to attract the eye into the window.

**Above**
French Connection's larger-than-life vinyl graphics dominate the façade of the London store and promote the season's trends.

**Above**
This impressive approach uses the store brand as part of the building's design at Uniqlo in Tokyo.

# Window calendar

**Large retailers will plan their window schemes well in advance using a window calendar. A well-planned window calendar will help a visual merchandiser organize window installation dates, ensure that each window has a scheme planned well in advance, and in many cases, it will help with budget allocations. In a reassuring sense, it will also help the visual merchandiser's job run smoothly. It is highly likely that a window calendar will be amended throughout the year; promotions can run longer than anticipated, and unexpected new products often need to have windows dedicated to them. However, a tentative plan will add some structure to the process.**

A window calendar is also a useful tool with which to communicate the workload for the year to others in the business. The buyers will want to ensure that the products that are to be promoted arrive in time. The sales staff will also want to make sure they have enough back-up stock available in their departments.

For decades, a visual merchandising manager would plan a window calendar using seasonal events as a backbone. In Christian countries, November and December would be blocked out to promote the festive season; discounted sales would (and still do) dominate two months in the year in winter and summer. Easter, Mother's Day and Valentine's Day are just a few occasions that often have window schemes dedicated to them. It might appear thoughtful to remind the public of such events, but it can also be naive to dedicate a run of costly windows to an occasion that only lasts one day and might only generate sales of low-priced items such as greeting cards. Instead, it would be better to promote gift-giving occasions that might encourage sales.

Today, however, with the greater competition on the high street, product promotions usually supersede many of the traditional seasonal events. With this in mind, it is advisable to be aware of which new product ranges have been bought by the buying department and when they are going to appear in store. Timings are critical for maximizing sales. It would be senseless to design a window scheme to promote new season collections if they are not present in the host department. At Selfridges, Alannah Weston prefers not to commit her windows to a year of schemes in case the fashion world dictates a new trend. "We work on only a six-month calendar because we like to keep the customer up to date with the fashion trends," she explains. "I do not like to commit to something a year away that might not be so topical when it finally arrives. If you plan too far in advance you can miss the point. We are a fashion business, whether it is apparel or home, and

**Above**
London's Fortnum & Mason traditionally presents elaborately themed Christmas windows. In this scheme, the front windows of the Piccadilly Street store were dominated by the tale of *Alice in Wonderland*. When the Christmas windows are dismantled in January, department stores usually start to plan the windows for the following Christmas. This allows time for research and design and the manufacture of props.

**Above**

This Christmas window from Harvey
Nichols in London features snowflakes
to produce a festive display.

we need to know what is out there in the fashion world. Attending the fashion shows is a great inspiration for me. Christmas, on the other hand, because of the vast amount of work involved, is planned a year in advance."

In the twenty-first century, many retailers now acknowledge global traditions and beliefs. Retailers may not only attract new customers by promoting them but prove that they, too, are worldly and aware of cultural differences. A Chinese New Year window or a Diwali window may also break the traditional appearance of a company's window displays.

An annual window calendar can start at any month of the year. Many retailers like to begin with Christmas, because those windows usually take the most planning and may need to complement the in-store seasonal decorations. Certain dates may be fixed and unable to move. It is always best to add these first to structure the calendar.

Once the proposed dates are added to the calendar, the task of designing relevant window schemes to support them can begin. To make things easier, the store windows should be numbered; the window numbers

can then be set against the dates. The visual merchandiser will thus be able to check at a glance on what date windows 1 and 2 are to be re-dressed, for instance. Large stores may have numerous windows that may not all be dressed with the same window scheme. Windows may be split up to accommodate several promotions, and numbering the windows will clearly define the window allocations. A comprehensive window calendar will also show precisely when an existing window is to be stripped and the time allocated to install a new one. Remember: the less time the window is in a state of undress, the better. Window-removal dates should be considered while preparing the calendar.

**Above**
Two spectacular Christmas windows from Bergdorf Goodman in New York. The intricate detail and dramatic colour schemes have turned these windows into three-dimensional artworks.

### Structuring a window calendar

Decide how long you want your calendar to run: six months or 12? Many retailers will even use an 18-month calendar.

Decide how you wish your calendar to appear. Many visual merchandisers will use a paper chart, yet others may use a computer program that can be accessed throughout the business. An interesting calendar can be produced using images and designs to demonstrate how the window schemes appear in reality over the allocated time.

Allocate windows for major promotions first: i.e. Christmas and sales.

Add secondary promotions: i.e. Easter, Mother's Day, Valentine's Day.

Use the free window spaces to introduce window schemes that may be product-related: i.e. new season collections.

Discuss with the buying/marketing team if they require window space to promote new departments or special events.

Allocate budgets to each of the window schemes. Remember that Christmas windows may justifiably attract a larger slice of the budget because they are generally in for longer and because the store may wish to compete with its rivals on the high street – every store wishes to be noted for outstanding window displays at this time of year. Smaller schemes that are not in for a long duration should not have large budgets set against them.

Design and plan the windows well in advance. Large schemes with complex props may need a lot of attention. Prop-makers have to be briefed and their studio time booked.

Always plan the removal of existing window schemes. On most occasions this should only take a couple of hours; however, complex displays may take longer and eat into your dressing time.

Completed windows can be photographed for reference later. This is best done at night with a black screen so that you won't get reflections. If you are freelance, take at least a quick snapshot for your portfolio.

**Above**
Kenzo sweatshirts appear to float down on to a frozen winter landscape in a Christmas window display at Selfridges, London.

# Window standards and maintenance, and budget

**To a few visual merchandisers, it may come as a sense of relief to have completed the task of dressing a window. Often they will not take note of their work again until weeks later, when they are stripping it, ready for the next installation. Unfortunately, this attitude towards their work will never gain them a good reputation.**

### Standards and maintenance

Window checks are laborious and time-consuming, but they are essential for maintaining the standards of a window display. Senior visual merchandisers often delegate this task to their juniors. Window checks should be completed early in the morning and at the end of the day. A notepad and pen and a scrutinizing eye are usually the only requirements. A checklist can be produced to ensure that any member of the visual team will look for the same problems or mistakes.

The most common faults include the following:

### Dust and dirt

Materials that hold static electricity, such as Perspex, will attract dust. There are sprays available that promise to help slow the build-up of dust; however, they will not prevent it. Surfaces and floors should also be checked for dirt and dust.

### Fallen props and products

Not only should the visual merchandiser check for obvious problems such as a fallen mannequin, he or she should also look for props that may have moved or slipped. Adhesives can either dry out or melt in the heat of the window, dislodging materials or fabrics.

### Fabrics

Draped fabrics can start to sag and begin to lose their effect after time in the window, and it is sometimes necessary to refresh them by adjusting and re-pleating. Coloured fabrics can also fade in the sunlight; it is always advisable to replace them if this happens; the faded colour might be misleading to a customer.

### Plants and foliage

Whereas artificial plants might look realistic to the consumer, dusty leaves will be a sure give-away. The leaves can be washed or wiped down with soapy water. Fresh flowers must be monitored at all times, depending on the fragility of the blooms; petals will drop and stalks will wither.

### Lighting

It is always advisable to scrutinize not just the dressing but the lighting too. Lightbulbs often blow and can leave parts of the window in shadow. In some cases, whole lighting tracks can short-circuit. Lamps and chandeliers used in the grouping may also need lightbulbs replaced.

### Heat

The heat from the sun combined with the window lighting will often melt candles. To prevent this, cut the candles as short as possible; without the length and the weight, they are unlikely to droop.

**Linda Hewson is Selfridges' Creative Director. Over the years, she and her team have produced many stunning displays that are often controversial and eye-catching. Here is her checklist for novices wanting to produce a successful window presentation:**

When planning the window make sure you clearly understand the concept or design, and know what budget is available.

Always produce a visual or sketch before starting to install any products or props.

Consider the space you have and what is physically possible; will everything fit through the door?

Decide where the main focal points are going to be.

Think about what products you will be representing. Who are you targeting and will the products be suitable?

Ensure that the props do not overshadow the product.

Be certain that any mannequins being used are sympathetic to the product.

Is it necessary to use graphics or ticketing?

Choose a strong colour palette.

If using props, ensure that they are made to a high standard and are finished well.

Remember: often the simplest windows are the best.

## Budget

Spending vast amounts of money on visual merchandising will only benefit the store if the visual merchandiser has the expertise to demonstrate effective visual merchandising. Expensive props and elaborate window schemes still need to be installed and dressed by individuals who understand the fundamental rules of layout and how best to use the space to create stunning displays.

Having said that, setting a budget against a visual merchandising project is a necessary part of the process. Remember: it does not always cost a lot to be creative. Many of the most effective window displays have been economical yet effective.

When setting a budget, it is often easy to overlook the main factors that will eat into your allocated amount of money; painting a window, for example, may cost more than expected when you take into account the cost of the paint, tools and painter. Signage and graphics can also be costly. Window-display projects may also require additional help from outside experts such as freelance dressers; in these cases, fixing a daily rate will help keep the work within budget. Of course, savings can always be made; a shrewd visual merchandiser will rarely discard used props or fixtures, as many can be recycled and reused (see page 72).

## The future

The future of window displays lies in the hands of the retailers. Selfridges' Alannah Weston believes that the public will never stop admiring windows and will continue to visit the high street for inspiration. "More and more, we need to open up our stores so that people can see in," she says. "That will obviously have an effect on the window displays of tomorrow; we are going to have to be very clever in how we approach it. Window displays, as in three-dimensional presentations, are always more effective than any plasma screen or two-dimensional presentation that I've seen; however, we have just recently seen a demonstration of a hologram machine that was very effective. If technology gets good enough, then we will use it – we are, after all, at the forefront of window displays. It's the same principle as questioning whether people will stop going to the theatre when they can get films on DVD. The experience and tactile nature of creative windows will always be more rewarding to view. Live models, movement and definitely sound is something that I would like to use in the windows. However, all of that will only serve to support the original art of window dressing that has been around since stores opened."

# Store study:
# Fortnum & Mason

In 1705, Hugh Mason owned a small shop in St James's Market, London. By 1707, he had been joined by his lodger, William Fortnum, and together they started a business that has lasted 300 years. Throughout the centuries, Fortnum & Mason has built up a reputation as the purveyor of fine foods and groceries, not only with members of the British royal family, but also with a loyal clientele, all of whom appreciate exquisite food. As Charles Dickens wrote of one trip to watch the horse race known as the Epsom Derby, "Look where I will...I see Fortnum & Mason. All the hampers fly wide open and the green downs burst into a blossom of lobster salad!"

The challenge for the visual merchandising manager at Fortnum & Mason is not only to create inspirational windows but to do so while keeping the shop's traditions in mind.

Paul Symes has the task of producing the F&M windows. His "Cabinets of Curiosity" window scheme for December 2006 lived up to the grandeur expected. Here, Paul talks about the inspiration, creation and installation of the F&M windows.

### Fortnum & Mason has a very eccentric, unique quality. How did you decide on the window scheme?

"Fortnum & Mason houses a veritable feast of delights, sourced from far-flung corners of the globe. In a similar way, in the eighteenth century, the appetite for knowledge led aristocrats to travel the world in search of undiscovered and interesting artefacts and objects, which they would then display in showpieces called 'cabinets of curiosities'. Eventually, the cabinets would become as diverse and eccentric as the artefacts they held.

I wanted to produce a scheme that not only conveyed the eccentricity of the store, but also allowed us to display an eccentric mix of product from all over the store. The cabinet of curiosities seemed to present the ideal showcase.

The cabinets had to be individual in themselves, with their own 'personalities', but at the same time they could not overpower the product that was to be displayed on them. They not only had to have shelves and features to group product upon, but also had to contain the displays within a specific area."

### How important is it to keep the Fortnum & Mason brand image in mind while designing the window scheme?

"The brand image is of paramount importance when designing a window scheme; the scheme should not only sit comfortably with the brand image, but also embrace it. This

**Above**
This style of casual grouping is used to maximize the space in the cupboard's shelves and drawers while retaining a focal point: the open drawer in the centre.

**Above**
Fortnum & Mason's "Cabinets of Curiosity"-themed windows were used to
display an eclectic mix of food and fashion.

knowledge influenced my decision to create this 'eccentric' window scheme."

### How long did it take for you to design and develop the window scheme?

"The design stage took a couple of days. Once I had thought about the initial concept, I then began to put my thoughts on paper in the form of simple sketches. I wanted to ensure that there was a common relationship between each cabinet, and that they sat comfortably alongside each other.

Then I drew more elaborate sketches, and began to add subtle details such as colour and embellishment. The whole process took about a week."

### How did you specify the windows for the prop-maker? How did you get your vision across to the prop-maker of how the windows should look?

"Initially we spent some time discussing my vision and feel for the scheme, but to a large extent the prop-maker worked from my original drawings. I wanted the scheme to sit comfortably with the products that would be displayed on the units, so we spent some time walking around the store looking at merchandise."

### What was the process of getting the window scheme made after you had briefed the prop-maker?

"As soon as the scheme went into production, I started making weekly visits to the production studio. This was my first scheme for Fortnum & Mason, so it was important that there were no nasty surprises on installation day. Each stage of the manufacture was monitored and signed off; sample paint finishes and embellishments were discussed and approved.

During each visit I would take photographs of the props so that we could converse over the telephone in between visits, with each party having a full knowledge of the detail under discussion."

### What do you consider when selecting the merchandise for the windows?

"Prior to selecting product for the windows, I hold a briefing session for all the store's buyers. This usually takes the form of a visual

**Above left, top to middle**
A hand-drawn sketch is produced as an initial idea. A more detailed drawing is produced to scale to ensure that the scheme fits comfortably within the dimensions of the window.

**Top right to below**
The window prop is near completion and has one final check before the paint, gilding and decoration are applied. The completed tree growing out of the top of the cabinet adds a surreal note to the final window display.

a member of the team assisting. The majority of the products for the window will have been chosen and cleaned beforehand, but as with all things creative, there are always ideas that suddenly come to mind on the day."

## Can you describe briefly the installation and timings of the window scheme?

"The design stage takes about a week. From there the production stage takes six weeks, and the installation of the props takes a day. It usually takes four days to dress a window run (eight windows), including lighting.

I like the scheme to simply arrive and be put into place. I don't want passers-by to see empty windows but something magnificent even before we have started to add the product. To achieve this, the scheme is usually installed on a Sunday morning, and the windows are cleaned, ready for dressing first thing on Monday."

## How important is the window lighting?

"Lighting can either make or break a window scheme, and very effective results can be achieved with inexpensive equipment. The most important rule is that it must be maintained and properly adjusted.

We have two basic systems in our windows: a high-level track with halogen wide and narrow spot beams for overall lighting, and a low-level track with low-voltage 20-watt narrow-beam spots for feature lighting. Occasionally we may use coloured lamps, gobo projectors or LED lights with changing effects. Each one of the fittings has an integral dimmer switch."

## How do you maintain the windows to ensure that they remain fresh?

"The windows are checked and maintained morning, lunchtime and evening, and cleaned on a daily basis. That includes any dust that may have accumulated overnight. They are re-dressed every two weeks with new prod-ucts. If the same person passes our windows on their way to work each morning and again each evening, they have seen the same display at least ten times in a week, which can seem like an age! I want people constantly to see something new, something that catches their eye. Our windows are never finished; they have always just begun."

presentation showing the development of the concept from the initial sketches through to the latest production stages.

During the following few days I visit each buyer to discuss the merchandise they wish to offer from their department, and start to work out how each product will feature in the windows, and I collect sample products to show the visual team. I then start to build up a mental picture of how the final windows will look: what colour will be prominent, what the secondary colour will be and the style of dressing we will use."

## How do you start the dressing process? Do you brief your dressing team beforehand?

"As soon as I have a clear picture in my mind of how the windows will look, I arrange for a briefing meeting with my team. At the meeting I will present the concept and show them the props, which will now be in the final stage of production. If time permits, some of the team may have visited the prop-maker and have seen the production themselves. I always dress the first window, usually with

**Above**
The lighting emphasizes the product, with pin spotlights used to highlight the three main groupings.

# In-store
# Visual
# Merchandising

"It is extremely important that we have an established theme that begins with our windows and translates to all areas in-store nationally. The in-store areas are just as important as our windows and provide our customers with information and entertainment."

John Gerhardt, Creative Services Director, Holt Renfrew

**In-store visual merchandising is the process used to lead customers through a shop in a logical order, encouraging them to stop at designated points and, hopefully, to make a purchase. Ask shoppers why their favourite store should stand so high in their estimation and many will probably explain that the space is easy to shop in, the product is simple to find and the signage is clear and informative. Each of these answers demonstrates effective in-store visual merchandising.**

As a visual merchandiser, your input into the merchandising of the store will vary depending on the type of shop in which you are working. In a small boutique, you may be called upon to refresh the layout in order to encourage customers to browse, and you will have a great deal of input into how this is done. In a multi-chain retailer, you will be more likely to be following directions from head office, which will often relate to buying programmes, store promotions and seasonal events. Specialist stores may rely on the visual merchandiser working with the buyers to lay the floor according to the new season's product and trends. Whichever type of store you are in, the same disciplines of in-store merchandising will apply.

Key to successful in-store visual merchandising is a successful floor layout. First you need to establish product adjacencies before you can start to plan your floor layout. There is then a series of options from which you can choose your fixtures and fittings, as well as some basic rules of product handling to help you display your merchandise effectively. Hot shops and in-store displays, and point of sale and add-on sales will help merchandise your shop. Signage and graphics can also help in-store visual merchandising, as can the creation of ambience. Finally, care and attention needs to be given to maintenance standards.

**Above**

A sculpture of a giant baby in the IT Beijing Market creates a sense of fun and drama.

**Below**

Not only has Lane Crawford, Hong Kong, created strong focal points to attract the customer on this men's floor, it has also added footprints on the floor to help guide the customer towards them.

# Product adjacencies

**The starting point is product adjacencies. This refers to which products sit next to each other: hosiery next to lingerie, kettles next to toasters and fruit next to vegetables. To maximize the space and use of the selling floor, the customer should be guided through the fixtures and aisles from one product to the next. By placing products that have empathy with each other, customers will not get confused and possibly pick up other items for which they may not have specifically been shopping. Clever use of product adjacencies will reinforce the appearance of the area and give it authority. A handbag fixture positioned next to scarves, gloves, hats and purses suddenly becomes an accessory department.**

### Making a rough plan

Before starting to lay out a floor, always check which product categories and brands are available to you to merchandise. The best and most effective way to start is by making a list. Taking a floor plan and tentatively noting where the products should sit will make the task more manageable. As well as product adjacencies, you might want to think about the location of strong product categories or key brands, which should ideally be positioned in prime locations. These brands and products will help the customer gain awareness of what the shop, department or space is selling and reinforce the strength and quality of the merchandise on offer. A wall of denim with strong branding, like Levi's for example, will make a statement and guide the consumer to the area where other brands of jeans are for sale. In the same way, a wall of pillows will inform customers that they are approaching the bedlinen department.

As well as product adjacencies and the use of merchandise to guide the customer around the store, the other area to consider is customers' comfort level. A boutique selling both men's and women's clothes could have the two ranges merchandised together. However, men might feel uncomfortable browsing through ladies' clothes to find their own; therefore a sensible approach might be to split the shop in two and dedicate one area to menswear and one to womenswear. The two areas would have to meet somewhere, and at this point the cash desk could be used to divide them, or you could feature products that could be classed as unisex, such as magazines, jewellery or T-shirts. Getting the product adjacencies incorrect could be costly to the store and also drive customers away.

Finally, if you are positioning named brands, it is best to understand where they see themselves on a floor plan. Large brand owners may have very strong views and have the clout to exercise them. Egos can clash when dealing with prestigious brands that will expect prime locations; their demands should never be overlooked. Many smaller brands, on the other hand, often wish to be placed adjacent to brands to which their customers aspire.

Once you have placed the product categories and brands roughly on the floor plan, you should visually walk the shop floor; the aim is for your eye to follow naturally from one category to the other.

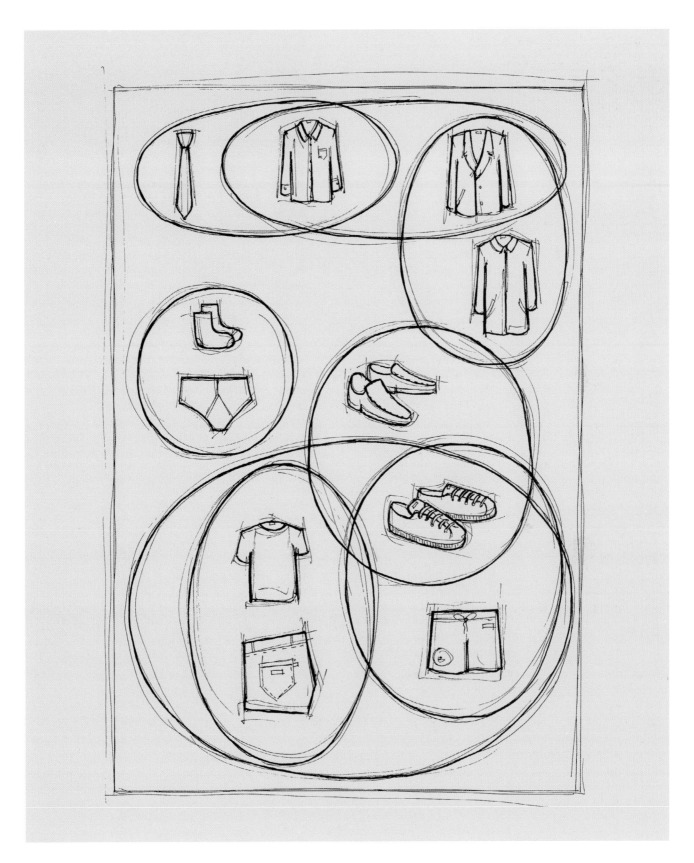

**Above**

Making a rough plan of the products that should sit next to each other is the first step in laying out a shop floor. This is called making the product adjacencies. Ties, jackets and suits or socks and underwear are two examples. Eventually, all the groups of product adjacencies will interlink to create one cohesive floor plan that contains them all.

# Floor layouts

**Once you have noted your product adjacencies, it is time to plan your detailed floor layout. Any shopper struggling to navigate the labyrinth of an IKEA furniture store will have noticed how difficult it is not to be tempted to leave the designated route. Once customers have entered the store, they have no choice but to traverse the shop to find the exit; while doing so they are led through numerous lifestyle room settings designed to offer inspiration, and then to a warehouse to spend. Even while queuing, their children can enjoy an ice cream. Few people would understand the ingenious planning that has gone into such a disciplined floor layout.**

Similarly, the countless aisles of shelves in a supermarket have been rigorously planned. While they may not inspire the customer, they do achieve their aim by making the monotony of grocery shopping effortless and uncomplicated. The exact location of the dairy products in relation to the cleaning products, for example, would have been carefully planned, not only to assist the customer but also to drive sales. Staples such as milk and eggs

are not always placed at the front of a supermarket for the customer's convenience; they are often located in the centre of the store or towards the back, ensuring that the shopper has to pass other items before discovering them. While searching, shoppers will probably add additional products, for which they were not necessarily shopping, to their baskets. Even the ends of the fixtures are used to make extra sales, often being used to promote offers. These invaluable spaces are usually placed along a central walkway with heavy traffic, making them a useful commodity to grab the shopper's attention – and money.

Each of these examples proves the power and effectiveness of a well-planned floor layout.

Fashion retailers selling both menswear and womenswear have the difficult task of deciding how to use their selling space effectively so that they can promote their products to both genders. Women are more confident shoppers, and will navigate themselves through menswear to reach their destination; men are not so confident, and prefer to find their purchases without trawling through dresses.

The easy solution would seem to be splitting the store down the middle, with men's and women's clothing easily identifiable. However, this does not often work because of space constraints, and many retailers want to create a whole-floor concept that suits the consumer and the merchandise. The ambience of the entire space or floor can enhance the product and make the shopping experience more exciting. The contemporary fashion brand All Saints has a winning solution: both men's and women's new arrivals are displayed at the entrance of the store so that both sexes are aware of the product mix, but then with strategic signage male customers are advised of the larger selection available towards the

**Above**
Neatly folded merchandise has been colour-blocked to make it easier for customers to shop in Primark, Bristol. Clearly defined walkways make it easy for the shoppers to browse.

**Opposite**
Milan's Corso Como features an eclectic mix of old and new furniture to display its products. Quirky lighting and art adorning the walls also help create atmosphere.

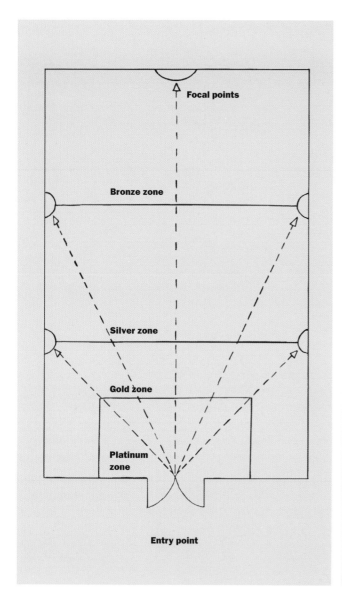

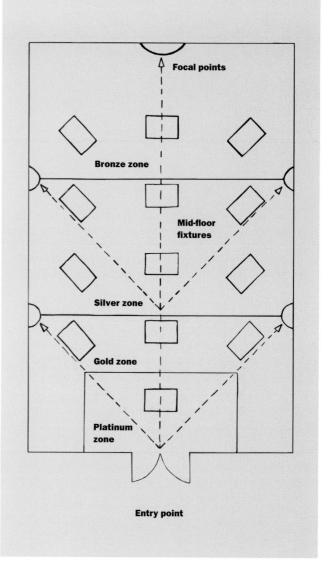

back of the store or on the first or lower-ground floor.

On the high street, menswear traditionally comes second to womenswear, purely because women spend more on fashion than men. However, because of their spending habits women will generally travel further in a department store to seek out a bargain or desirable item. It is not unusual for menswear to be on the first floor and womenswear on the floors above, with cosmetics and fragrance dominating the ground floor. The concept of a beauty/fragrance hall is a model used in department stores worldwide. Not only are these items desirable in their own right, but also one should not ignore the vast amounts of marketing invested in them: every magazine will feature the latest skincare phenomenon and "must-have" fragrance. This is also a shrewd way for a department store to enhance its brand offer online and in-store. The retailer may not carry Tom Ford's latest fashion collection, but if it sells his fragrances it can list the designer as one of the luxury brands it carries. It is no secret that most designers make huge profits by franchising their brand through cosmetics, sunglasses and underwear. It suits both the designer and the retailer to position such products in prominent places.

**Above left**
The floor layout here clearly shows the most profitable platinum selling space inside the entrance to the store. This area will be expected to take the most money, followed by the gold, silver and finally bronze areas at the rear of the store.

**Above right**
The same floor layout is shown here with fixtures in place. Each fixture is angled at 45 degrees to funnel customers into the store. Fixtures are also placed in line with displays on the side walls, which create focal points that are designed to attract customers into and through the store, encouraging them to explore the whole shop.

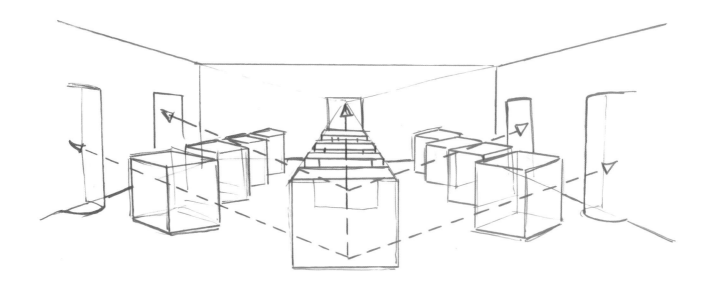

### Platinum, gold, silver and bronze areas

The key to laying out a floor is the positioning of products. Visual merchandisers often divide the floor into four areas and define these by colours: platinum, gold, silver and bronze (other retailers may use numbers or letters). It is important to comprehend that the first area of the store when entering is the prime selling space; this is why it is called the platinum space. The second as you walk through the shop is called the gold area; the third towards the back of the store is silver, and finally the area at the back is bronze. The first thing to note on your floor plan is, therefore, the entrances, as they will determine where the customers enter and exit the store and thus the position of the platinum area. The lower-priced, sale, promotional or high-fashion items should be positioned in the platinum area, as this space will always attract more customers and more sales. The bronze area at the rear of the store will draw fewer customers because of the distance from the main entrance; with this in mind, it is best to place some staple products or a desirable brand or product category there to encourage customers through the store.

In addition to using product placement to attract customers into and through the store, the most significant consideration when laying out a floor is to lead the customers through the platinum part of the store to the designated points where they can be encouraged to browse and spend. If this is done, customers will remain longer in the store, and the longer customers are in the store, the higher the chances that they will make a purchase. In order to keep them content, their shopping experience should be both trouble-free and enjoyable. Clear directions and walkways will guide them and good product presentations will help them decide what to buy.

A strong brand will act as an anchor to a floor and pull potential customers into a particular area of the store.

**Above**
An elevated view of the same floor layout looking in from the entrance. This shows how the eyes should easily focus first on and then through the fixtures to rest on the focal points.

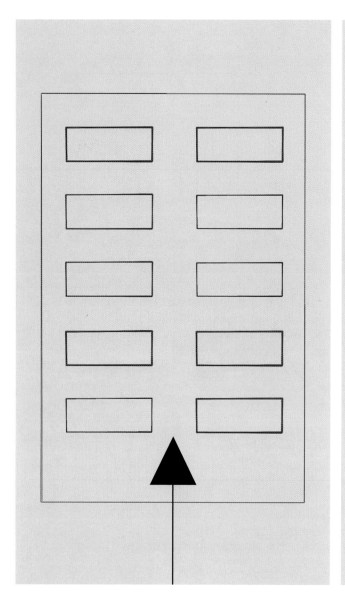

Chevroning is useful on large floors where there is plenty of space. In smaller stores, however, keeping all the fixtures straight and square to the walls will create the illusion of space.

## Footfall, walkways, sight lines and focal points

A key factor that should be considered before laying a floor out is "footfall". This term refers to the route a customer walks through the store – or preferably the route the retailer wishes them to follow.

On entering a store, customers will be challenged with several decisions: do they go left, right or forward or decide to leave? Assuming that they stay, it will be the retailer's task to help them choose which way to walk around the store. Sight lines and focal points will encourage them to explore the shop.

Sight lines are imaginary lines that lead the customer to certain areas or specific products. Focal points can be an in-store display, a collection of carefully arranged merchandise, or a display featuring a key brand that immediately catches the eye. A focal point is best used in conjunction with the sight lines. Once the customer's eye has followed a sight line, it should comfortably rest on a focal point. It is therefore important that sight lines are not obscured by large fixtures or walls.

**Above**
In the first illustration, the fixtures are placed in regimented rows at right angles to each other. This type of arrangement can form a barrier, discouraging customers from moving through the store. By moving the fixtures to a 45-degree angle, as shown in the second illustration, they can be used to funnel customers through the store. This is often called chevroning.

Customers may be steered through the fixtures by defined walkways that act as sight lines. Many of these paths are designed to stand out physically from the rest of the floor, either because they are a different colour or are made from a different material from the rest of the flooring. However, such defined walkways can also act as a barrier; many nervous shoppers subconsciously do not like to leave the comfort of the walkway. It is for this reason that it is possible to have walkways that are not defined; many stores have one universal floor covering, and cleverly position the fixtures to funnel the customers through the store. Fixtures or tables should, however, not be positioned so that they become obstructions or barriers. They should also be placed far enough apart that pushchairs, wheelchairs or other mobility aids can be manoeuvred easily between them.

Another feature that can be used to attract customers into and through a store is the walls. Linear (wall) space is a vital part of any shop. The walls surrounding the store can hold a vast amount of products without eating up valuable shop-floor space. If key brands or strong product categories are positioned on linear fixtures, the customer will see them and walk through the store towards them.

## Positioning the products

With the above techniques for attracting customers into and through the store in mind, and referring to a product adjacency list, you can now start to lay out the floor plan and decide where best to place the products. Always start by placing the largest categories and key brands first: they will undoubtedly take up the most space and, hopefully, generate the most sales. With the adjacencies in mind, the next step is to fill in the gaps. One key factor to remember when doing so is the need to vary the pace – to create gaps between products or to introduce a different type of fixture, for example. This will keep the customers' attention, preventing them from becoming bored if every rack of clothing looks the same, or even overwhelmed if there is just too much crammed into the space.

**Above**
In another form of floor layout, in the womenswear designers' gallery in Selfridges, London, a lack of defined walkways is counteracted by the use of fixtures to break up the floor space and create customer flow.

## Overall style of the floor layout

The style of the store's layout will depend on the products you are selling and what feel you wish the store to have. A designer boutique specializing in expensive garments may justify a spacious contemporary feel with minimal dressed fixtures. A womenswear store may benefit from a feminine feel, while a menswear store may work better with harder lines and darker colours. A gift shop may lend itself to a more densely filled emporium with fixtures placed closer together. In this case, the key is to give the appearance of a generously filled store without making it look clumsy and busy. Large fixtures are best positioned towards the perimeter walls unless they are specifically designed to break up an area. Tables can be a useful addition to a shop fit if they are merchandised correctly (see page 137). If you are using the walls to house branding or signage, it is important that it does not encroach into important linear selling space and that it is relevant to the product either beneath or in front of it.

Display areas should also be considered when planning the floor layout; remember that an in-store display may look appealing, but it will take up precious retail space. A group of mannequins might not get the same monetary return as a table of seasonal products. It is always wise to question if the floor is taking on more of the resemblance of a showroom or museum than a shop. Customers will not interact with the products if they feel they should not touch them. Attaining the right mix of fixtures to display is essential in creating customer comfort.

Finally, consideration should be given to the cash desks and changing rooms. If they have not already been positioned, think about placing a cash desk at the back of the store in the least profitable area (bronze). This is not only a commercial decision, but will act as a tool to draw customers into and through the store. Changing rooms are also best sited at the back of the store. Stores with particularly attractive and portable merchandise that may be pilfered will benefit from having cash desks at the front of the store as well as towards the back. Although there are no guaranteed ways of preventing shoplifting, positioning staff at the main exit may act as a deterrent.

**Above**

SSUR's Shanghai store has the appearance of a stately home, yet sells men's streetwear. The juxtaposition of traditional and contemporary has been carefully considered to enhance the brand's identity.

**Opposite**

With traditional floral wallpaper, original period fireplaces and an opulent chandelier, Stella McCartney's perfumery department in London has the appearance of a boudoir and gives the store a very feminine touch.

# Store study:
# Matthew Williamson

British designer Matthew Williamson
graduated from Central Saint Martins,
University of the Arts, London, in 1994.
His creativity was noted by Italian
design house Marni, where he worked as
a freelance designer. He then moved to
British retailer Monsoon and Accessorize.
Not content with working under the
constraints of others, Williamson
launched his own collection of couture
fashion in February 1997. His success not
only as a designer but also as a retailer
has made his collections desirable to the
rich and famous. His clientele includes
A-list celebrities such as Beyoncé and
Kate Moss. He opened his first stand-
alone store in Mayfair's Bruton Street,
London, in March 2004 and has since
opened stores in New York's fashionable
Meatpacking District and recently in the
Dubai Mall, Dubai.

Williamson's eye for detail stretches further
than his embellished and colourful designs
that are seen on the catwalk – he has been
able to translate his innovative design
concepts into his store design. His stores
boast vibrant hues, exquisite detail and a
huge amount of embellishment.

### How important is store design in the twenty-first century? Do you feel that it helps to promote a brand's identity?

"I opened my first store in London in 2004.
Until then I had to be content with having
people view my collections within spaces that
did not reinforce my design aesthetic, or at
least complement them. Having a custom-
designed space is a powerful tool for any
brand; it delivers the whole lifestyle, which
allows people to comprehend fully what the
label is about. Opening stores in New York
and Dubai undoubtedly helped shape people's
perception of the brand and bolstered our
reputation in the territory."

### Your store design has complete empathy with your clothes. Was it challenging to design stores to showcase your work?

"Designing stores has definitely been a
labour of love. With each one I wanted to
create a space that fused together elements
that I habitually use as themes within my
collections to ensure that they were displayed
in an engaging way. The challenge came in the
translation of those themes from fashion
design into interiors without being too literal,
but I am happy with the balance I found.
For example, the intricate embroidery and
beading found on MW garments is reflected
in the delicate vintage brooches that adorn
the wallpapered areas of the stores and within
the changing rooms."

**Above**
The exterior of Matthew Williamson's store is simple but elegant. Once inside,
the customer is led into different themed areas, each one characteristic of
Williamson's brand.

**Above**
An indoor exotic garden is the centrepiece of Matthew Williamson's London
store, creating ambience and a sense of theatre.

The Dubai store was also heavily influenced by the region. The rotunda and punched starred ceiling are examples of this, as is the domed section of the store. I wanted to reflect not only the culture of the surrounding environment but also take some inspiration from traditional craftsmanship, as demonstrated in the intricate fretwork."

### How did you ensure that the colourful and detailed designs of your stores would not overshadow your collections?

"When working with bold prints and a vivid colour palette there is a danger of allowing them to become overpowering within the space. However, I feel that the stores achieve a happy balance, with accents of colour or embellishment within more neutral spaces. I also incorporate a lot of mirrored surfaces within the stores, which open up the space to disperse the feeling of being overwhelmed."

### Did you have a vision of how your stores should look? What was your inspiration behind the store design?

"From a very early age I had a clear idea that my store would have a fuchsia-pink sign above it, but other than that my ideas were undefined until I had chosen the first store space. The London store concept evolved organically in some ways, with aspects of the building itself – such as the natural light well at the rear of the space – inspiring the encased tropical jungle.

The New York and Dubai store designs took inspiration from their immediate surroundings while retaining the brand's signature as dictated by the first flagship.

In New York, the industrial feel of the Meatpacking District is evident throughout in the clean line and through the materials used such as the poured concrete flooring. Here, as with London, the design was influenced by the very building itself. The space here is long and narrow and punctuated by a central column of iron supports. Instead of fighting against them, we embraced them as markers of smaller, cocoon-like rooms within the store. The result was a store design that draws customers on a journey through the space and one that also allows for greater freedom in merchandising, or for highlighting certain parts of the ready-to-wear collections.

### You are renowned for your confident use of colour and prints. Was this a major design factor that you considered when planning your first store?

"I wanted to explore the juxtaposition of old and new in the materials with which I chose to furnish the store, so we have antique Venetian glass chandeliers hanging above neon signage. This idea of unexpected combinations is also encapsulated in what I call 'hyper-nature', where the synthetic meets the natural. I used the existing pale and powdery marble flooring of the building as a contrast to the oversized, bold-pink till area for a striking focal point in the space. Elsewhere, traditional deGournay chinoiserie wallpaper was dramatized with accents of neon, which I personally handpainted."

### You have produced some crazy window displays. How does a dinosaur devouring a mannequin in one of your dresses promote sales? (I loved the window, by the way – very clever!)

"The window displays are something I have always been proud of, and I have a team of inspired people who work with me to generate these wonderful displays. I think that in their essence, the displays are there to capture the imagination of passers-by and encourage them to notice both the store and the

**Above**
Williamson's trademark indoor jungle acts as an impressive backdrop to his New York store.

garments. Matthew Williamson customers are defined by their confident nature and a sense of flamboyance in their personal style, and they would appreciate the tongue-in-cheek approach."

### Do you think that mannequins are useful props to carry your collections?

"Live catwalk shows will always remain the best way to showcase a collection, but realistically a mannequin is the most appropriate option for in-store. Hanging garments rarely convey the nuances of a cut or fit of a piece."

### You always take time to install a complete window scheme. How important are your window displays?

"I direct a team, but as the London store is very close to my studio I often participate in the installation itself, too. The window displays are extremely important to any brand because they are the first impression a client has of the store and the collections. It pays to be flexible in changing installations to suit external or seasonal factors."

### How often do you install a new window scheme?

"We install new window displays around key points in the year to signal to customers that a new range is in, or simply to celebrate fashion week or the winter holidays."

### Whose stores do you enjoy shopping in?

"There is a real sense of theatrics to Kokon To Zai on the Goldborne Road, and I love the fact that this haven of eccentric goods is housed in a former run-of-the-mill butcher's with the Victorian decoration still intact and very much made a feature of. The mixture of taxidermy, contemporary fashion and macabre objets d'art is truly an assault on the senses.

Also, true to its name, the variety of designers and artists who are represented in Dover Street Market give a marketplace feel, offering unexpected finds every time I visit. The atmosphere is very inspiring and the strong personal vision of Rei Kawakubo is perceptible through the store."

### What's next for the Matthew Williamson brand and store design?

"Spring 2011 sees the introduction of the first men's collection for the brand, so I will be looking at ways to incorporate a specific area into each of the stores to house it. The stores all have a feminine feel to their design, so I am looking forward to the challenge."

**Above**
Dark lighting and a sophisticated colour scheme are the theme for this area, which includes a dramatic panel with a contemporary lighting installation.

# Fixtures and fittings

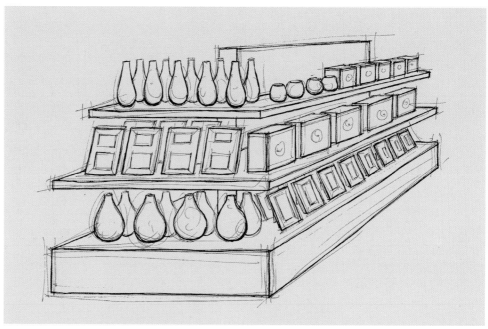

Once you have planned the final store layout, it is time to select the fixtures that will be needed to house and present the merchandise. The use of the correct fixture is paramount in producing sales. Selecting the correct fixtures may at first seem daunting. Choosing a structure that holds the correct number of products and shows them to their best advantage is never easy. There are two universal styles of fixture that most retailers will use: mid-floor and linear. They can be used in conjunction with each other and both come in various forms.

## Mid-floor fixtures

A mid-floor fixture is free-standing and can be used not only to carry merchandise but also to steer customers through the store. They can be shopped from all angles, making them a useful merchandising commodity. Ideally they should not be so high that they obscure other areas of the store. Their proportion should also suit the products they are housing; small items may get lost and look insignificant on a large fixture. There are many different types of mid-floor fixtures, ranging from purpose-built gondolas to tables and found items. Some of these are more suited to displaying fashion and some to homeware, while many can be used for either purpose.

**Above**
This three-shelf gondola is typically used to house homeware items. Larger items are ideally placed at the bottom and smaller ones at the top to achieve visual balance. The centre of the top shelf can be used for signage.

**Above**

The Maison Martin Margiela store in Nagoya, Japan, makes great use of its high ceilings. White bust forms are positioned theatrically above head height, and the product is displayed below so that it is accessible to the customer.

**Gondola Uses**

Homeware:
candles, vases

Food:
pre-packaged items

Special occasions:
Valentine's Day gifts, Christmas

## Gondolas

A gondola fixture is most commonly used in home and food stores. Gondolas can be any size, but most are rectangular and have shelves on all four sides. The ends are referred to as gondola ends or end caps. The shelves are often adjustable, making them flexible and able to house most product categories. Gondolas can be repositioned on the shop floor, provided they are easy to move. Many have lighting built into them and will require an electrical socket to be positioned nearby, ideally under the unit. Themes and stories (see pages 60–68) can easily be presented using gondola fixtures. It is important never to use too many different products; a clearly defined offering will have more impact. It is wise to remember that a gondola fixture should be filled to its capacity – it is a selling tool, not a display instrument. Retailers often stock the lower shelves with smaller items that are more difficult to make a strong selling point with, or create a group of products on the top shelf that may be easily tampered with. Larger items should always be placed at the bottom of the gondola, with smaller items at the top. The lowest shelf should be at least 30 cm (1 ft) off the ground; customers should not be expected to stoop to shop. Many gondolas have slots at the top where signage can be placed. The signage should just simply state what the gondola is carrying.

**Above**
A selection of free-standing gondola fixtures has been used to display books and art materials at Cass Art in London. They have been placed apart from each other, so that customers are able to view the items from all four sides.

## Tables

Tables used as merchandise fixtures can be purchased or bespoke. They are an interesting way of breaking up a floor and are easily browsed. It can be a good idea to place a lower, smaller table partially underneath a higher one, creating two height levels that will give more impact than one. Customers often feel comfortable shopping from a table because it is an object that will be familiar to them in their homes. Folded garments or items of homeware suit tables best. Clothing items should not be stacked too high; one of each size will generally suffice. A half-mannequin or bust form can be used to show the item of clothing displayed on the table. Homeware items may be piled higher. It should be remembered that tables are high-maintenance: they will need constant attention to keep them presentable.

**Above**
Murano glassmaker Carlo Moretti displays his wares in minimally merchandised displays on tables, creating a gallery effect that shows the quality and design of the glass to its best advantage.

**Below**
Folded items sit above a rail of jackets in the men's formalwear area of Karl Lagerfeld's London store. A glass cabinet positioned mid-floor houses valuable accessories.

**Furniture Uses**

Homeware:
folded items such as bedlinen, china

Hanging items:
capsule collections of clothing can be hung in wardrobes

For smaller cabinets:
jewellery

**Found Object Uses**

Flat surfaces:
an antique table can be used to display traditional china

Plinths:
can be used to display vases or pieces of sculpture

Trunks:
can be used to display blankets, bedlinen, cushions or boxed gifts

Baskets:
can be used to contain scarves, umbrellas or small homeware items

Glass mid-floor fixtures will always appear lighter in an area than solid wood ones.

## Furniture

Cabinets and cupboards are often used to present merchandise. They can be used to create theatre while also functioning as a useful selling fixture. Jeans, for example, can be neatly folded and placed on the shelves of a cabinet, as can homeware items. A cabinet can also be chosen to coordinate with the merchandise: china could be placed in a glass-fronted display cabinet, while a capsule collection of clothing could be hung in an open wardrobe. It is wise to remember that a cabinet may have an unattractive back to it that is best hidden by the back of another of the same size. Care should be taken to light the merchandise inside a cupboard because it is enclosed. It can be tricky to do, so it is sensible to ensure that there are sufficient overhead spotlights to focus on the product, or even to add under-shelf lighting.

**Above**
These simple free-standing fixtures in Dover Street Market, London, are not used to show products but to create an exhibition of macabre items. They encourage customers to pause in the shop and then hopefully look at the merchandise around them.

**Below**
Found objects including antique chairs, cabinets and chandeliers work alongside contemporary clothing and mannequins to create the eccentric style of London's Dover Street Market.

## Found objects

Trunks, crates and plinths are just a few found objects that can be used to present merchandise. They may have nothing in common with the majority of the other fixtures but can often change the pace and appearance of parts of the store if utilized well, such as antique pieces used alongside contemporary fixtures to provide contrast. They can also be cost-effective and may be recycled, too. It is important that found objects are there to serve a purpose; a personal favourite from home is not acceptable unless it can help sell. A shrewd retailer will also mark these items up and sell them, thus providing the opportunity to replace them with other original pieces.

**Above**
These traditional glass cabinets in Baccarat's showroom in Paris take on a modern twist, with lighting breaking through the glass ceiling from a huge suspended boulder of crystal, demonstrating the quirky style of the designer, Philippe Starck.

Housing expensive crystal, the cabinets are enclosed and secure, but allow the customer a 360-degree view.

### Vendor fixtures

A vendor fixture is given by the supplier to the retailer to house and display the vendor's branded products. These fixtures can be either permanent or temporary. The advantage of using a vendor fixture is that it will not cost the retailer anything, and will be designed to carry that specific product and in the correct quantities, adding brand recognition for the customers. Retailers will often have no choice but to use them if they wish to carry the brand. Such fixtures can, however, be a hindrance. Although they may enforce the brand name, they may not fit in with the store's appearance. A branded fixture is, however, best used to its full advantage and not hidden away; hiding or disguising fixtures in dark corners will not fool the customer and will only alienate the vendor.

### Branded shop fits

Like a vendor fixture, a branded shop fit will enforce the brand image and be designed to complement the products. Sometimes known as shops-within-shops, or concessions, the product is supplied by the brand and not bought by the host store. Carefully selected by the host store and with regard to the correct product adjacencies on the floor, these shops-within-shops can enhance the overall floor layout and help to change the pace of and improve customer circulation, maintaining the interest of customers as they work their way from shop to shop. Many retailers will use them as an anchor for the whole floor; a prestigious brand will certainly grab shoppers' attention if placed in a prominent position. Seasonally, a branded shop fit can change dramatically; a designer may insist that the store changes its appearance to suit the collection by adding different graphics and signage and by remerchandising the area.

### Concept shop fits

Many retailers that specialize in one specific product or style of merchandise push the boundaries when designing their stores. Most of these retail environments have become concept stores that rely heavily on the following of their loyal customers. A concept store should be designed with the product in mind, with bespoke features, and strong branding and graphics.

**Above**
Offspring's concession in a department store features product-specific fittings, including wall fixtures designed to hold individual shoes, low mid-floor fixtures that are easy to shop from and seating for customers to try on trainers. In-store concessions will have their own loyal fans. Offspring customers visiting the shop-within-shop might then be tempted to purchase from another concession within the store.

**Above and below**
Supreme is a skateboarding shop
in Los Angeles, with a loyal customer
following. Their store includes a
half-pike to test the skateboards; this
also creates a dynamic atmosphere.

### Specialist fixtures

Certain products will only lend themselves to specialist fixtures. Fresh produce that needs to be refrigerated will often need a specifically designed fixture. Although an open-fronted chilled fixture may not be aesthetically pleasing, it is still essential that it performs well, and products can still be arranged in a creative display. Chiller and freezer cabinets should also be designed so that they can hold large quantities; the owner of a sandwich shop will expect to sell a lot of stock over a lunchtime, so having to restock a cabinet constantly would be senseless.

Ribbons, beads and fresh flowers, to name a few, need some considerable thought as to how they are best displayed. Beads, for example, because of their size, will need to be positioned close to eye level so that they may be viewed comfortably. Ribbons may need to be measured and cut by the salesperson and should be easily accessible for this purpose. Fresh flowers obviously require water; buckets may be disguised inside purpose-built shelving or display units.

Any product category can be merchandised effectively if consideration is given not only to the product, but also to the customer.

**Above left**
A natural-wood shop fit for paper products creates a tactile experience in this Prints store in Singapore. Three types of display are used: cards are placed upright; writing paper is set on angled shelves; and gift boxes are stacked onto wall fixtures.

**Below left**
Specifically designed to display rolls of ribbon, these fixtures, as used by VV Rouleaux in London, are accessible and easy to maintain with their curved shelves.

**Above right**
Bespoke wall fixtures have been designed to hold the latest mobile phones in this Orange store in Paris. The design of such fixtures requires investment and should be thought through at the same time as the store's architectural concept.

**Above**
This innovative way of displaying both cycles and clothing, as used in Chain Reaction, Belfast, creates an interesting showcase for both types of merchandise. The cycling trend can easily be coordinated because they are enclosed in their own futuristic pods.

**Below**
The futuristic design of this optician, l.a.Eyeworks in Los Angeles, gives the impression of cleanliness amid a technologically advanced environment. Atmospheric lighting, clean lines and mirror-backed glass shelves are used to promote the latest eyewear, while the mirrors also serve as a practical tool for customers trying on the glasses.

## Hanging rails

Rails designed to hold garments come in many sizes and shapes. They can be purchased from wholesalers or made to order. There are two basic styles that can be used: capacity and single-bar rails.

### Capacity rails

A capacity rail, as the name implies, is a capacity fixture designed to show many options of garments and carry a large amount of stock for a high product turnover. They are usually made from metal and have several adjustable arms that hold the hangers in position; they can be shopped either from two sides, known as a T-stand, or four, known as a quad rack, or they can be hung on a wall as part of a wall fixture (see page 146). It is worth thinking about the height at which the arms are set – if they are too high they may be harder to shop. The products hang facing the customer; smaller sizes should be placed at the front and larger ones at the back. They are best utilized to show just one style of garment in many sizes, or items that together make up an outfit, like a jacket and trousers. Since they are easy to replenish, large multi-chain retailers often favour them. They are also easy to manoeuvre and can be repositioned to suit the products.

**Above**
Here polo shirts are displayed on four-prong capacity rails at Topman in London. Each prong holds one style in several sizes. Smaller sizes should be hung at the front and the largest at the back.

### Single rails

Stores selling more expensive clothing often use a single running rail, no different from a conventional running clothes rail. The single straight rail is best used to show fashion collections or a trend theme. They should not be overstocked; leaving one to two finger widths of space between each hanger is ideal for the customer to remove and replace garments easily. Colours should always run from left to right along the rail, starting with the lightest. Sizes should also start with the smallest on the left, progressing to the largest on the right. The hangers should all be the same style and shape, with the opening facing away from the customer; in this way the garment will be easy to remove and replace.

### Circular rails

Circular single rails, positioned in the middle of the shop floor, were fashionable during the 1970s and acted in the same way as a straight rail. Today they are frowned upon, appearing clumsy and offering no flexibility. However, they can be useful for presenting one piece of discounted merchandise through its spectrum of different colours, such as T-shirts.

**Single Rail Uses**

One type of garment

A whole collection

Sale items

**Above**
Three single rails positioned against a plain wall help create an eye-catching display area for a designer collection in Dover Street Market, London.

# Wall fixtures

**Not only can a well-merchandised wall produce great sales, but it can also be used as a backdrop for a specific product area. Some systems are more flexible than others. Many retailers favour an arrangement that can offer as many options as possible. Smaller boutiques often incorporate the linear fixtures into the store design and so may not be so concerned about being able to change the configurations.**

## Slat-wall and grid systems

Large multi-chain retailers often use a slat-wall or grid system because of the flexibility each can offer. They are generally designed and used to show high-turnover products because they can be replenished easily. Best used for showing fashion garments, they can also support shelves for homeware items or to support a display above eye level. There are various components that can be purchased and used with these systems, such as prongs, rails and shelves. There are many options for prongs available for all types of fashion items. The most common is the waterfall prong, which holds more than one item; these are available either as a horizontal or angled-down version. The bar itself features spacing nodules, which hangers can sit in or against. A straight arm without spacing nodules will hold more merchandise because the hangers will not be spaced. Both are available as round, square or rectangular. Many retailers build up a kit that they draw from when required.

A slat wall is made up of panels of wood that are painted or laminated and fixed directly onto the wall. The components simply slot into the gaps between the strips. A grid wall consists of a sturdy wire grid that also fixes directly to the wall, and the bracket clips onto it. Neither system is particularly aesthetic when stripped of its merchandise. It is always advisable to ensure that the brackets are placed close enough together so that when the product is hanging from them, the system is hidden. Ideally a slat-wall or grid system should be painted the same colour as the wall, enabling it to blend in with, and not overshadow, the product.

## Fixed rails

A fixed sturdy rail that carries fashion garments will always look smarter than a rail supported by a slat-wall or grid system. However, remember that they will not offer the same flexibility. A strong metal or wooden rail is often supported by wall brackets at each end of the pole. It is imperative not only that the pole is strong enough to take the weight of the garments, but that the brackets are, too; winter clothing in particular can be heavy.

**Above**
The use of side-appraisal and folded
items on the table for Dries Van Noten
helps to show the many clothing
options. The dressed bust form on the
shelf can easily be changed to
promote new items or trends.

## Fixed shelves

As with a fixed rail, a shelf securely attached to a wall offers no flexibility but may be visually pleasing. A shelf may be attached using brackets that are used as a design feature, or by an invisible bracket that is screwed to the wall with the shelf casing slid over it, concealing the hardware. Walls with natural alcoves suit shelving; planned carefully they can create interesting merchandise areas. Shelves can be constructed from various materials, including wood, metal, glass and acrylic. Consideration of the product should be taken into account when introducing shelves to a store. If they are to carry weighty items, a glass shelf may not be appropriate as it may break. Acrylic shelves are prone to scratching and may warp if overstocked. Wooden shelves are best laminated or lacquered; handpainted gloss paints or emulsions will scratch easily.

Lighting shelves can be difficult; the deeper the shelf, the more shadow it will cast on the shelf below it. Ceiling spotlights can be aimed at the shelved wall; however, the lower the shelves, the less light they are likely to get. An alternative is under-shelf lighting, which can be fixed to wooden or metal shelves.

**Fixed Shelf Uses**

Homewares

Fashion items

**Opposite**
Stylish fixed shelving throughout the Alexander McQueen store in New York is used to exhibit ladies' accessories in this high-end fashion store. Concealed lighting is incorporated into the underside of the shelves.

**Above**
Nike has cleverly created valuable linear selling space in its store near Phoenix, Arizona, by designing free-standing fixtures that not only divide the department but also display products.

# Product handling

There are numerous ways to
merchandise both mid-floor and wall
fixtures; some of these are more suited
to walls than mid-floor fixtures, and vice
versa. Gaining a knowledge of these
basic principles will aid any newcomer
to visual merchandising.

### Colour blocking

Using the colour of the product to create
visual impact is the simplest and most
fundamental way of presenting any type of
merchandise. From T-shirts and towels to tins
of paint and crockery, each product category
can create a functional yet bold display. The
skill of colour blocking is by no means difficult
to master. This style of product handling is
low-maintenance and easy to replenish. It is
often favoured by large superstores and
high-street chains and can be applied to both
wall and mid-floor fixtures.

### Horizontal merchandising

This style of merchandising is best suited to
wall fixtures. Merchandise is hung or shelved
in horizontal rows. Each shelf or row of the
fixture may be arranged by colour or by the
same style of product item, such as a row
of floral T-shirts or a series of square vases.
Ideally, one product per row is better than
several. This style of presentation is
functional and easy to replenish. It is worth
noting that products placed at either the top
or the bottom of the fixture will not attract the
same attention as those placed at eye level.

**Above**
Knitwear in neutral tones is displayed
from the top to the foot of these
shelves in Uniqlo's store in Tokyo.
Smaller sizes should be placed at
the top and larger at the bottom.
Top shelves that shoppers cannot
reach can hold extra stock.

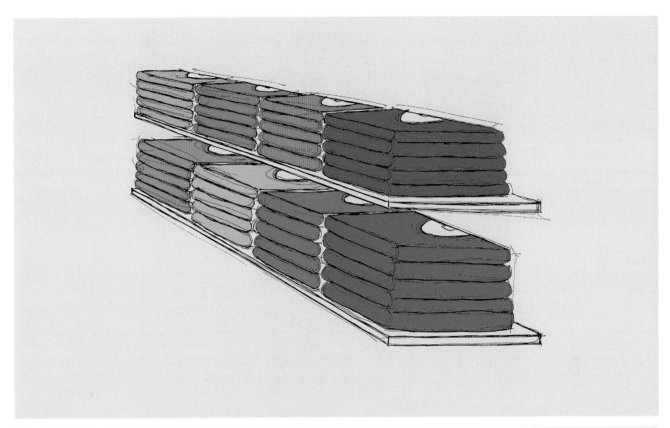

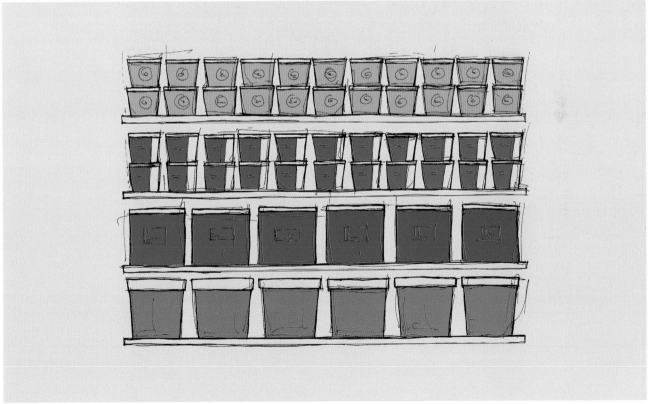

**Above**
Colour blocking is one of the simplest and most effective ways to display products, by grouping items by colour. It is easy to maintain, replenish and shop and can be applied to both fashion and homeware.

**Below**
Horizontal merchandising is a simple term for products being shelved or hung horizontally from left to right. Larger items should be placed at the bottom and smaller ones at the top. It is important that shelves or rails are positioned as close to each other as possible so that there are no gaps that could weaken the impact.

It is good to utilize basic rules of colour grouping. However, many collections today are designed with key trends in mind, in which case plain or neutral colours may integrate better with the look.

### Vertical merchandising

As with horizontal merchandising, this format uses lines of products, but this time running from the top to the bottom of the wall. It can be used to show the different product options available and can be merchandised by colour. As with the horizontal format, this style is easy to replenish and is functional.

### Product blocking

This style of merchandising is best used for volume merchandise. Generally, a fixture or wall is stocked with just one product category or range. Product blocking shows authority and creates impact. The use of this style of merchandising is logical for the customer because it shows the colours and sizes clearly. Product-blocked fixtures are low-maintenance and easy to replenish.

### Symmetrical merchandising

As the name suggests, symmetrical merchandising is a style of presenting the product to create a mirrored effect. This method is only suited to wall fixtures. The product is presented in the same way on each side, with an imaginary line running vertically through the middle. Symmetrical merchandising will require more wall space than would be necessary to show a complete product range, purely because the same product is duplicated.

**Above**
Vertical merchandising is the display of product from left to right and top to bottom and, again, is suitable for clothing or homeware. It is also easy to replenish and shop.

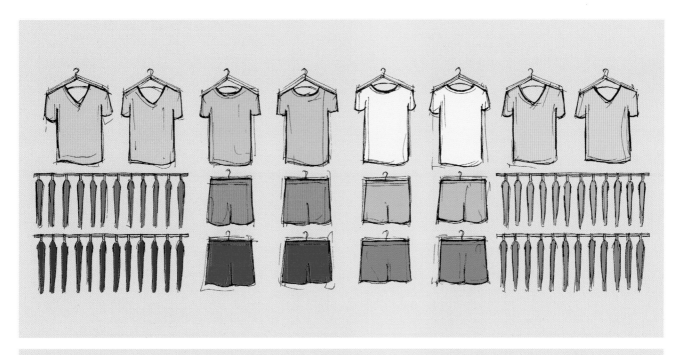

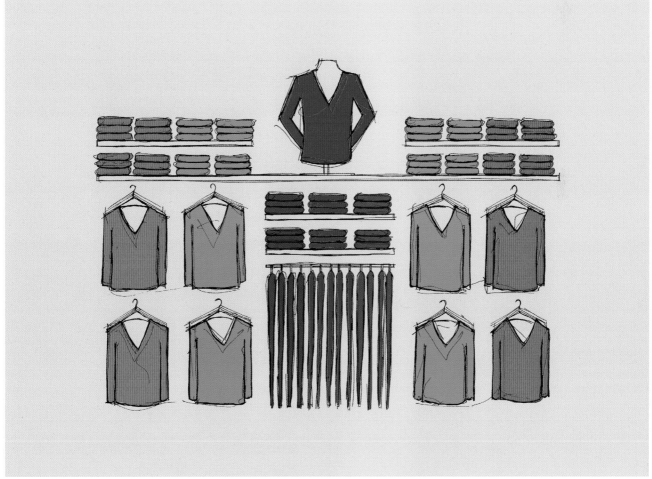

**Above**
Product blocking is used here in a layout for men's T-shirts and shorts. Prongs have been used to show front-facing items, and rails used for products hung in profile. This type of display is efficient for fast-turnover products, especially for fashion items.

**Below**
Using a wall fixture with shelving, prong and rail components, products are displayed symmetrically. This type of display is easy to create and is pleasing to the eye. The bust form can be used to draw attention to the display or to highlight an item of clothing.

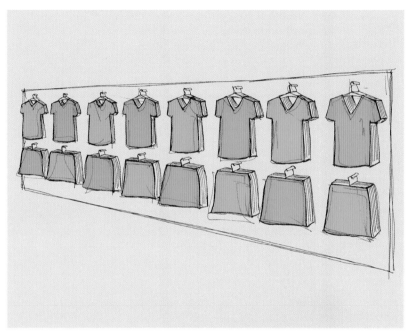

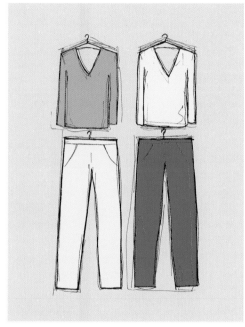

### Chequered merchandising

Chequered merchandising is effective and
easy to execute on wall fixtures. It relies on
the use of colour to create impact. Like a
chequer-board, products are alternated along
a length of wall. The overall effect should
be balanced and symmetrical.

### Anatomical merchandising

This style of merchandising is only suited
to fashion items. The idea is to hang the
garments on top of each other in the same
way they would be worn: i.e. shirts under
jackets. Anatomical merchandising creates
complete, defined looks and can be used
for mixed product types.

**Above left**
An effective use of wall space that
relies solely on the merchandising
to produce the effect, chequering uses
two colours alternately to create a
chequer-board pattern. This is useful
for enlivening basics such as T-shirts,
school uniforms and knitwear.

**Above right**
Whether on a wall or mid-floor fixture,
anatomical merchandising is used to
display fashion items where garments
are displayed as they would be worn –
such as a top displayed above trousers.
This type of display can be used to
inspire a look or a fashion trend.

## Coordinated merchandising

Fashion or homeware category groups benefit from using the coordinated merchandising technique. Collections or themes are grouped together to create a cohesive look. A jacket would be hung with a coordinating shirt and could be accessorized with a coordinated tie. A sofa could be displayed with a coordinated cushion, rug and throw, placed on or around it.

This type of coordinated merchandising can also be applied to homeware. To create a coordinated look, you might put cushions, curtains, throws and associated soft furnishing products together, depending on their style or trend; a traditional floral print could be broken up with plain knits and traditional stripes to create a French Provençal look, whereas muted greys and naturals could be highlighted with accent colours, such as bold pinks, reds or blues, to create a contemporary look that would suit an inner-city warehouse apartment. These looks are designed to give the customer inspiration and educate them on how to put products together.

## Displaying product collections

The alternative to coordinated merchandising is to show collections that demonstrate the authority of the range in-store. Instead of dispersing candles throughout the home floor, coordinating them with textiles and ceramics, they can all be housed together to create an authoritative selection of varying colours, sizes, styles and price points. This will give customers a clear understanding of the range of candles on offer but leave them to make their own selection.

**Above**
Coordinated merchandising is the art of placing products together in the hope that customers will buy more than one item. The aim is to create a "look" for them. Here at Dover Street Market in London, shoes, dresses, jackets and coats are on display.

# Store study:
# Flight 001

**Flight 001 is a unique concept store specializing in travel goods and catering for the jet-setter's every need. The founders, Brad John and John Sencion, interviewed together here, both began their careers in retail and design.**

Their first store in New York drew attention from both the public and the media. Now with stores across the USA and in Dubai, Flight 001 is gaining international recognition.

Every design detail has been considered, from the overall shells of the stores, which resemble the interior of an aircraft, to the linear and mid-floor fixtures and the strong graphics that reinforce the brand's identity. The diversity of the collection ranges from keyrings to suitcases, and care has been taken how best to display each item. Because of these details and the product mix, Flight 001 remains an innovative concept store.

## Your store is very product-specific. Was it challenging designing a store that has to show so many different product categories?

"Yes, it has been challenging but it is something we enjoy doing. Our store design has been an evolutionary process, beginning with the first prototype where we made some design decisions about rounding the corners in the space but designed only one fixture: the ticket-counter register. Before opening our first store we didn't know the characteristics and dimensions of all our products, so by the time we opened the next store two years later, we knew that we needed to create adjustable shelves for the side walls. In the third store we made an attempt to figure out the centre-floor fixtures, but it wasn't until the fourth store that we perfected them. We have now addressed all our product categories and are currently working on smaller display fixtures for all these products."

## Was the overall store design important?

"The overall design of the store was extremely important. When we opened our first store in 1999, 'design' per se was a dormant faculty for the general public. It was only after the turn of century (and millennium) that the idea of 'design' as a concept was awakened and came alive. Back in 1999 we felt it was a differentiating decision not just to throw paint on the walls and open a store. At the time our attention to a store design concept made us different. Design was an option then, but today design is not an option when opening a successful store – it's a must."

## How did you decide on the complete look for the first flagship store?

"Our travel concept has always made decisions easy and entertaining for us because it is so focused and directed. We use travel as a

**Above left**
Flight 001's concept travel stores are designed to resemble the interior of an aircraft fuselage. Because the store is open-fronted and the customer can look straight in, it is important that the interior is always merchandised to a high standard.

**Above right**
For a store that is solely reliant on the travel customer, luggage is a key product category. A lightbox with a retro graphic of a case is placed dead centre on the back wall, thus pulling the customers through to the luggage area at the rear of the shop.

metaphor when making design, brand, and 'terminology' (language) decisions, so an international airplane lounge was an obvious inspirational choice for our store prototype."

## Has each of the fixtures been specifically designed with the product in mind?

"Absolutely. We have several fixture options based on our broad product assortment. We have a general area on the side walls consisting of adjustable shelves. These shelves include back-stock storage bins at the very bottom. Centre-aisle showcases are used for more expensive, smaller items. We have an essentials peg wall used to merchandise smaller, unattractive products that we repackage, and in the back of the stores we have the same adjustable shelving without storage bins that we use for luggage and large travel bags."

## How do you decide the overall layout of the store's products?

"We have a centre runway aisle that makes it easy for customers to get from the front to the back of the stores. When we originally put the store layout on paper, we used zones to identify certain areas based on the departments we thought would be important, as well as the product adjacencies.

The cash desk acts as an anchor to the store and is designed not to overshadow any of the fixtures or product. Even the front of the cabinet has been glazed to house expensive items such as watches. A low table opposite does not crowd the space for waiting customers, and the wall behind it has not been heavily merchandised so that the area is free for customers around the till."

## Are the product adjacencies important in driving sales?

"Yes. We think of adjacencies as 'suggestive selling'. So, if you are buying personal-care items, you might consider placing a groom bag to carry all these products right next to it."

## Do you use any vendor fixtures? If so, do they work with your brand aesthetically and practically?

"It is always a challenge to use vendor fixtures because they often don't have the same design aesthetic we have within our store.

We do use vendor fixtures when they are functional and in line with our brand."

## How important is signage to your stores?

"Signage is our dialogue in courting our customers, so it is very important. The challenge is making signage unobtrusive but meaningful.

The true meaning of concept is an idea, a thought or a notion. With this in mind, it is always worth considering why a store may be considered a 'concept' store. Having twice as much merchandise in a larger space does not qualify, nor does designing an elaborate shop fit to carry a collection already available in other stores. A true and successful concept store like Flight 001 has an interesting product mix, innovative store design and a retail ethos that helps support the brand and sustain customer interest."

**Above**
The design of fixtures to work with the product is very apparent in the Chicago store. Enclosed glass display cases are used for small, high-value items, while adjustable open shelves carry the bulk of the merchandise. Drawers resembling overhead lockers are used for storage.

**Below**
The merchandising of the shelves is carefully conceived, with colour blocking used for bags on shelves on the left-hand side. The placement of a lower fixture adjacent to or opposite a higher one gives the impression of space and does not crowd the entrance to the shop, or block the smaller items in the shelves behind it.

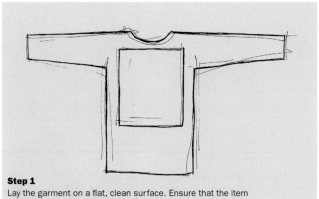

**Step 1**
Lay the garment on a flat, clean surface. Ensure that the item has no creases. At this stage, tissue paper may be placed on the garment. Place the folding board on top of the tissue or directly onto the garment.

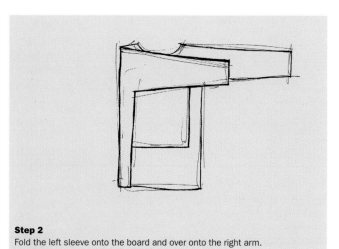

**Step 2**
Fold the left sleeve onto the board and over onto the right arm.

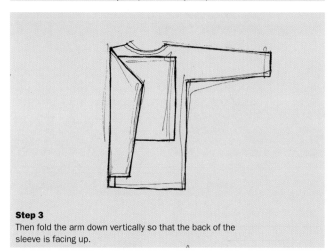

**Step 3**
Then fold the arm down vertically so that the back of the sleeve is facing up.

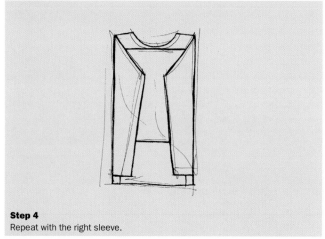

**Step 4**
Repeat with the right sleeve.

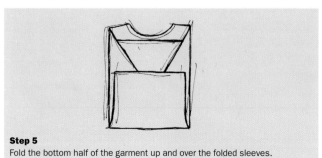

**Step 5**
Fold the bottom half of the garment up and over the folded sleeves.

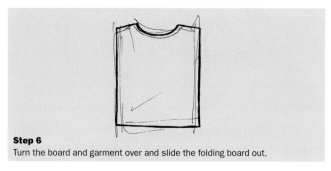

**Step 6**
Turn the board and garment over and slide the folding board out.

## Prepping fashion items

Depending on whether a retailer uses wall fixtures or mid-floor fixtures, all product items, whether fashion, homeware or perishable goods, will still need to be presented correctly. This is known as "prepping".

Hanging garments should be unpacked and "prepped" – and ideally should follow the useful guidelines opposite.

## Folding boards

A folding board is a useful tool that will enable anyone who is folding clothes to make certain that all the folded items will be the same size. They are, however, only useful for folding knitwear, T-shirts and shirts. They are usually made from either wood or Perspex, and can be made to suit the size of specific shelves.

**Above**
Folding boards create great results for folding tops, such as T-shirts.

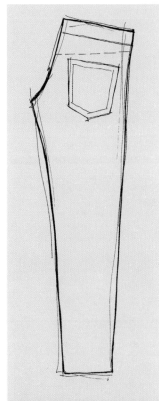

**Step 1**
Fold the trousers (without folding board) into themselves so that both the back pockets are visible. Lay the folded garment on a clean surface. Ensure that the item has no creases.

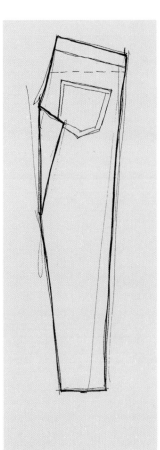

**Step 2**
Fold in the "seat" of the trousers so that the outstretched garment appears straight.

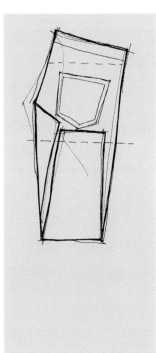

**Step 3**
Take the end of the leg and bring it up to just below the back pocket.

**Step 4**
Then fold the garment in half again.

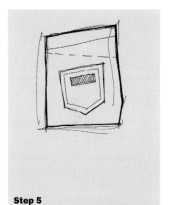

**Step 5**
If the item has a branded ticket on the back pocket, this should be clearly visible.

**Erin Thompson, former head of visual merchandising for Selfridges, London (now Vice President and Artistic Director of Coach) employed strict rules for the fashion floors that she oversaw. Her tips are:**

Items should be ironed or steamed.

Tickets should be attached to the label, or where least likely to mark the garment.

Alarm tags should be placed through a seam in the garment.

Hangers should be hung on the rail and all facing the same way.

All merchandise should be in size order, starting with the smallest items.

Merchandise should be grouped by colour categories.

Jackets and tops should be shown in front of trousers.

Ensure all of the shelves are clean and dust-free.

All tickets should be tucked into the garment so that they are not visible.

Keep similar products grouped together.

Make sure that a maximum of six to eight items are stacked together.

Ensure that all of the stacks of folded product on a shelf unit are the same height.

A folding board should be used for tops.

**Above**
Trousers are best folded using the above technique, for which folding boards are not used.

## Non-fashion merchandising

Merchandising homewares or solid products differs from merchandising apparel, yet many similar techniques can be applied. If the product being displayed is to be taken directly to the cash desk by the customer, the general rule is to ensure that the collection appears authoritative and that there are sufficient amounts available; a customer purchasing plates may require only one or a whole set. Exclusive, expensive items should not be duplicated or their perceived value will be diminished. Understanding the correct quantities to show depends on the selling price and the expected turnover. Volume products can, however, be stacked high and will look appealing, especially during sale times.

Food items can also benefit from visual merchandising theories and practices. Many types of fruit and vegetables can benefit from colour blocking. Yellow, green and red peppers, for instance, look visually stronger when grouped together by their colour. By piling their produce high, market stallholders attract customers by demonstrating their

product authority. The high turnover of the merchandise would not suit a minimal presentation, which may send a mixed message to consumers, telling them that the produce is highly priced because of the minimal presentation. Expensive caviars and fine wines, on the other hand, would clearly benefit from a simpler presentation; the customer on this occasion would want to be assured that these items are rare and not available to the mass market.

**Homeware products will also need prepping. Bear the following guidelines in mind:**

All products should be cleaned.

Sticky price labels should be placed on the bottom of each item.

Clear Perspex sheets should be placed in between stacked merchandise to help stabilize the product.

Products should be grouped in colour categories.

Items should not be stacked so high that they are difficult to shop.

**Above**

Dark, low-level tables are used to show home accessory items in the Globus Food Hall in Zurich, Switzerland. They have been sparsely merchandised to give the impression of exclusivity. Overhead lighting is positioned over the tables to highlight the products.

**Above**
What could be just a plain dividing
wall in Colette, Paris, has been
transformed into a strong visual
statement that leads the customer
into the store. The glass cubes holding
footwear have also been lit to highlight
the product.

# In-store displays and hot shops

"As a luxury retailer, it is paramount that we position like-minded and style-sharing vendors within the same space. Price points and brand cachet are essential considerations."

John Gerhardt, Creative Services Director, Holt Renfrew

**In-store displays can be straightforward; nevertheless, there are a few guidelines that will help the presentation be more effective. Hot shops are an invention from the 1980s that is still popular today. Both are designed to attract customers and sales and work in a similar fashion.**

### In-store displays

The idea of either continuing the window scheme in-store or presenting a selection of products with their own theme has been used by the large department stores since they first opened. In-store displays are created to continue the theatre and drama inside the shop. Usually they consist of products supported by props arranged so that they can be admired but not touched or dismantled and taken to the cash desk. On rare occasions, they may be designed not to sell products but to inspire; a piece of art or an art installation may not be profitable but will cause excitement and provoke opinions about the store's brand.

In-store displays should be created with the same care as window displays. The same layout and design principles apply, except that the displays are usually seen from all angles. Most in-store displays benefit from being raised so that they may be viewed from across the store without obstructions. A strong wooden base or plinth will help elevate the presentation. Like a window display, the plinth may need to be covered or painted to coordinate with the theme. It is important that the plinth is sturdy enough to support the weight of the display; a thick wooden top is best so that it can have produce or props securely screwed or nailed onto it. Electrical sockets can also be incorporated into the structure. A permanently positioned in-store display plinth will also profit from having a fixed ceiling grid discreetly secured above it with an effective lighting track.

**Above**
Oversized flowers dominate Tsvetnoy Central Market in Moscow, Russia. The colourful floral sculptures are perfectly scaled to the size of the store, and help to lead customers to the top floor.

**Above**
This in-store display in Niketown, London, is visually powerful and simply says "football"! The use of mannequins in repetition is not only eye-catching but helps promote the concept and the product.

**Below**
Mannequins interact with neon branding at Topshop, London. The strong poses and clever positioning of the models make this in-store display innovative, as well as serving to promote the season's fashion trends.

The main intention of all product displays is to sell. In-store displays should be used to pull customers into the store and get them to browse. If designed well, they should act as an inspirational guide. The most common use of an in-store display is to demonstrate to the customer which current trends and key looks are on offer in their host department. They are best positioned at the end of sight lines and should be used as focal points (see page 126). If a display is dressed with products from the host department, it is essential that the merchandise used is not far away. It would be senseless to create an eye-catching presentation using products that cannot be easily found. Positioning the product fixtures

adjacent to the display will encourage customers to spend purely because they do not have to look far to find the items they admired on the display.

In-store displays can also be used as a tool to inform the customer of other product categories available in the store. A furniture display placed at the foot of an escalator on the fashion floor of a department store can show the customer what else is available in the store and, with effective signage, can direct them to the location.

Maintaining in-store displays is, unfortunately, a task that will require time and patience. Many an exhausted customer has been found sitting on display plinths, often leaving discarded rubbish among the product groupings. Children are wont to climb up and swing from the props, and the merchandise, no matter how high, will be tampered with. Morning and evening checks will not be sufficient to keep the display pristine; encouraging the shop-floor sales staff to assume ownership of the displays can often help.

**Above**
A line of immaculately dressed mannequins elevated on a fixture and all wearing neutral colours make an impressive in-store display at Lane Crawford, Hong Kong.

**Below**
Female mannequins are suspended at different heights at Saks Fifth Avenue in New York, helping to create visual impact as well as showcasing the latest trends.

## Hot shops

As with an in-store display, a hot shop is designed to create interest and inspire the customer. In this case, however, more emphasis is placed on the product and not the props. A hot shop basically contains topical products, either by trend or look. Hot shops are often seasonal mini-shops-within-a-shop; they work by promoting a new idea or collection of products grouped together, often with a small display to help reinforce the look.

The difference between a hot shop and an in-store display is the fact that the customer is encouraged to shop from the former. A good example of a hot shop would be a beach shop. Because of the seasonal implications of selling beachwear, the retailer only has a limited time to advertise the product. To give the story more impact, various other product-related categories such as sunglasses, hats, sandals, sarongs and suntan lotions could be merchandised with the core beachwear. Mannequins dressed and accessorized in the relevant clothing could be positioned in the centre of the merchandise fixtures to promote the hot shop. Together, the complete collection can be given a name, and a brand can be created for the limited time that it is present on the shop floor. For the customer, a hot shop helps solve many shopping requirements; a woman planning a holiday can be informed of the seasonal trends and can find most of her clothes and accessories in one place without having to search throughout the store.

Home and leisure stores rely on hot shops more than the consumer might imagine. Again, mostly based on seasonal activities, the retailer will often create themes out of new product and place them at the front of the store to encourage sales. An outdoor dining theme consisting of barbecues, garden furniture and accessories could be placed at the front of a store in the summer months.

Christmas and other major festive dates all benefit from hot shops to help promote products. Christmas decorations that clearly have no fixed department for the rest of the year can either be grouped en masse in one area, or be split over several hot shops, each one with a different theme, such as contemporary decorations in the young fashion department and traditional decorations on the homeware floor. It is important to remember that hot shops can take up a lot of space. The department hosting one will need to be informed in good time; not only will it need to accommodate them on the floor, staff will also need to adjust their figures to compensate for the loss of floor space that the hot shop has taken.

**Above**
A hot shop in Debenhams, Liverpool, UK, uses mannequins to demonstrate the look and trend, while the products are positioned adjacent to them, making it easy for the customer to shop.

# Point of sale and add-on sales

**Many retailers maximize their sales potential by using point of sale and add-on sales. Both are aimed at customers who have already purchased and are now being encouraged to buy other items.**

### Point of sale

Anyone paying for a magazine in a newsagent's or paying for their fuel at a petrol station would have been targeted – on most occasions unwittingly – by point-of-sale merchandise. The fixture that holds low-price items such as chewing gum, batteries and air fresheners are all point-of-sale fixtures, usually supplied by the vendor. The power of point of sale should not be underestimated; this is the last chance the retailer has of taking money from the customer. Volume sales at low prices can be instrumental in elevating the store's sales turnover.

Destination stores such as a newsagent's will usually use point-of-sale fixtures supplied by brands that are designed to carry only their products, such as chewing gum. The brands are often familiar to the customer and are a useful commodity. Point-of-sale offers in department stores may not be as obvious. There the most common point-of-sale item might be a gift voucher or economical collection of merchandise. For a major retailer, the most profitable point-of-sale item would be for a customer to sign up for a store account card at the cash desk.

### Add-on sales

An add-on sale differs from a point-of-sale offer because it is generally driven by the sales staff. Retailers will often encourage their staff to try and persuade the customer to buy extra products that complement their main purchase, i.e. shoe polish or protectors for footwear sales, batteries with electrical sales and additional flattering cosmetics in the beauty hall. Not every customer is comfortable with this hard-sell technique, and it is sometimes wise to incorporate both add-on and point of sale to gain the maximum transactions. Positioning add-on sales close to the main product categories allows customers to discover them by themselves.

**Above**
Placed adjacent to the tills in the queuing area, sweets and small pick-up items are positioned to easily tempt customers. Debenhams, Liverpool, UK.

**Above**

In all UK Pret a Manger stores, crisps, biscuits and healthy snacks are deliberately placed near the cash till to tempt customers to pick up additional items. Many cash desks will have shelves specifically designed to sit at the front.

# Clearance merchandise

### Clearance lines can be presented in numerous ways:

Reduced goods can be pulled together and placed at the front of the store, enabling the customers to browse through them and then walk farther into the non-sale items in-store.

Sale goods can be used as a magnet to draw customers to the back of the store, leading them past the non-sale items.

Individual departments can use selected fixtures to hold sale lines.

Larger stores, like department stores, have been known to dedicate a whole floor to sales goods, usually on the least profitable floor (often the one farthest away from the main entrance), especially when the sale has finished and there is remaining discounted merchandise that has to be sold.

Large chain stores often rely on completely separate discount stores branded under their name to move sale lines or overstocked products.

**Clearance merchandise should not be overlooked. Sale times are extremely profitable for retailers. Most major stores will proudly present their discounted products twice a year and benefit from the rest of the high street following suit and thus attracting customers to the area. Many stores continue selling items at a reduction all year round.**

It is important to understand the store's philosophy and requirements when approaching mark-downs. Many retailers hide their mark-down offers towards the rear of the store, as if they are ashamed of them; others will proudly display them in the platinum and gold areas, hoping to generate on-the-spot sales, which can be more effective. Sometimes individual departments may have sale items when the rest of the store does not. In this case, a department can also adopt this process by placing the sale items at the front or back of the department.

### Sales signage

It is worth considering how you wish to promote the reductions at sale times. Many retailers like to show the original price and the corresponding reduction next to it. Many also like to show the percentage saved in the sale for the customer. It is unwise to use all of these methods on one ticket, however, as it may become confusing. Once your sale signage strategy is decided, it is best to apply the same approach throughout the whole store so the customer receives just one overall message.

Many shrewd retailers often add a phrase in small print on the tickets, such as "up to xx per cent off" or "many items at xx per cent off". This is not illegal in many countries, but it is wise to check with local trading standards offices beforehand.

**Above**
Covering the windows with vinyl is an effective and powerful way of projecting Selfridges' sale message in London.

# Signage and ticketing

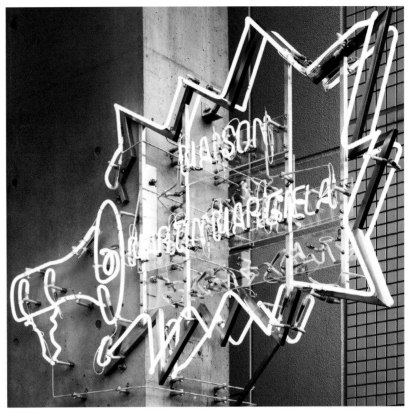

**Nowadays, signage is not just limited to handwritten or printed information. Neon, plasma and LED displays are some of the more modern innovative ways of communicating with the customer. Whichever style of signage a retailer chooses, it is important to understand that, whether the store is large or small, customers need to have explanations, directions and information made clear to them.**

## Store guides and other navigational signs

Before customers begin a shopping experience, they often wish to orient themselves. A large store with many floors needs to have detailed store guides and product locations. Often, this information is posted just inside the main entrance or at an information desk so that the customer has time to study the store's layout before entering. Complicated store guides will only confuse consumers; it is advisable to keep the directions simple but informative. A scaled-down plan of each of the floors with key destination points such as lifts and escalators will best aid the customer. Highlighting entrances, fire exits, restaurants and toilets can also orient and reassure the shopper. A printed leaflet of the store guide can also be either handed to customers on entering or placed close to each entrance for shoppers to pick up themselves.

**Above left**
A simple neon light sign becomes a prop in itself in the hands of a mannequin at Lane Crawford in Hong Kong.

**Above right**
Neon lighting reinforces the Maison Martin Margiela brand in the company's store in Nagoya, Japan.

# Case study:
# Colorset

Tom Phelan, interviewed here, and Frank Baptiste established Colorset in 2002, and opened their first design/print studio in Waterloo, London, with four staff. Today they have expanded their business to London Bridge and Nottingham so that they can service the whole of the UK. They now have 45 staff, including designers, creators and installers, and their clients include some of the most influential retailers, such as Burberry, Kurt Geiger and Mont Blanc. They have also produced graphics for airlines and major property-development companies, and for the London Olympics in 2012.

Colorset is noted for its outstanding service. Because it has design, production and installation teams working together under one design house, it is able to carry out projects across the UK, Europe and the USA.

### What type of signage and graphics are retailers asking you to produce?

"Mainly vinyl for windows and large-scale graphics as backdrops for window schemes. We have also been producing graphics for plinths used as part of in-store displays. A lot of our work involves producing light-box graphics, predominately for perfumery companies."

### Do you see trends occurring in your trade?

"Overall the trend we see at the moment is 3D work. We are frequently asked to produce props made from polystyrene because it is light and can be either sprayed or covered in vinyl. We have just produced an impressive isometric window scheme for Ted Baker using this technique."

### How does the design process work, from the client's initial brief through to installation?

"Clients often produce visuals that we develop and present back to them. Depending on the skill of the client's design team, we can often go straight to the development stage. We do, however, need to consider the scale of each of the windows that we are addressing; often we have to rework the client's designs so that they will fit within the constraints of the window. Clearly all windows are not the same size."

### What are the benefits of large-scale graphics for a retailer?

"The turnaround time from design to installation is exceptionally quick. They also create an amazing instant impact. The diversity of materials available today means that the store staff can be trained to install graphics themselves – they are now very user-friendly."

### Your team not only designs and produces signage and graphics but also installs them. Is this challenging to coordinate globally?

"It's like managing two separate industries. Designing and producing graphics is relatively straightforward, because we can take control within our central studio. However, installation is a specialist trade, and having to coordinate and send installers across the globe at short notice can be challenging. The logistics of sending a team out to install window graphics, working unsociable hours, often through the night, can be difficult. For example, window decals will not adhere to glass if the temperature is lower than -4 degrees C (25 degrees F)."

### How has modern technology affected the production of retail graphics?

"Technology has made printing a lot quicker, mainly because of the software and apparatus that are available. Printing machines can now print faster and to a higher resolution, and they can print on to a wider canvas. For example, we have just produced a graphic measuring 25 by 5 m (82 by 16 ft) that was installed in one piece. Design files can now be sent immediately via the Internet instead of having to be burned to a disc."

### Which design-software package do you use to design effective graphics?

"We mostly use standard design packages, such as Adobe Photoshop, Illustrator and InDesign, that are available to everyone."

**Above**
A decal has been applied to the glass of the window of GAP in Tokyo sending a message to the consumer. A decal can be custom-made and easily removed; a quick win for any retailer.

**Above and opposite**
Large-scale print has been used not only as in interesting backdrop but also to
endorse the brand's advertising campaign at Miu Miu in Tokyo.

## Which of your projects have been the most challenging?

"We once took on a very challenging project that involved creating a three-dimensional aluminium 6-by-6-m (20-by-20-ft) light switch that was positioned on the hoarding of Boots the chemist in Piccadilly Circus, London. The idea was that it was the main switch for the world-famous colourful illuminations. The overall effect was amazing! The team had only four days to produce the large prop and install it through the night, which as you can imagine was challenging on a rowdy Friday night in central London."

## In what innovative ways are you employing technology instead of mainstream print?

"Through Motion Advertising Technology (MAT), we are now able to transform window displays into interactive screens that can be any size. This means that the store window can stream media and social networking, and even allow the consumer to order merchandise from the street, turning the store into a 24-hour retailer.

Retailers are always searching for innovation, and we have produced interactive kiosks and motion-sensing graphics. Directional, interactive graphics are now used in shopping centres around the globe rather than traditional printed text, since these new formats can be updated easily at little cost.

We are currently working with Office shoes to develop an interactive window: when a customer places their feet on the pavement graphics, their image will appear on the window wearing the shoes they have selected.

Another major part of innovative marketing that we are exploring is 3D mapping. This involves taking exact measurements of a building or structure so that a moving image can be projected on to it. The effects are incredible. A whole building can come alive at the press of a button; synchronized with sound, the whole experience is breathtaking."

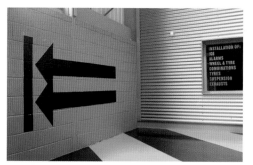

Once inside, the customer may need extra help to navigate the store. Often, signs – commonly referred to as banners – are hung above walkways. Banners are usually screen-printed or have vinyl text applied to them. They can either be cut from foam board or wood or made from coated fabric. Free-standing signposts placed at the beginning of walkways, escalators and lifts are also an effective way of telling customers where they are and what else is available in-store.

Departmental signage will help the customer plot a course around and through the merchandise. A strong supplier brand can act as an anchor to reinforce the department's product category. Used correctly and as a focal point, a strong brand on a wall will pull the customer into the heart of the department. Wall signage is an integral part of store design and visual merchandising. When used correctly, it not only directs but

also attracts the customer. Plasma screens and neon are a quirky way of creating theatre, yet confirming a message; they both can be used to add movement to bland wall fixtures.

Free-standing signs that are used to inform the customer of promotions, events or costs should always be printed on card and ideally be displayed in a Perspex holder. Sign-holders can be made to any size, but one universal size is usually more effective. Where the sign may be viewed from both sides, two can be placed back to back, or the sign may be printed on both sides. Signs in Perspex holders should sit with the product and be an integral part of the presentation, not an afterthought. Customers often move free-standing signs, and an easy solution is to fit the sign-holder to flat surfaces with double-sided tape.

**Above left**
The success of this sign in Heal's store in London lies in its simplicity. The size of the lettering means that it is easily spotted across the shop, enabling customers to find the department easily and also drawing them across the floor.

**Above right**
Two bold arrows direct the customer around this Halfords car-maintenance, enhancement and travel-solutions store. The use of colour and graphics is also reminiscent of roadway signs to relate to the motoring aspirations of its customers.

**Below**
Strong graphics have been employed at Sainsbury's, London Colney, not only to promote its collection of flowers but also to remind the public that Mother's Day is approaching.

## Text and colour

Directional in-store signs should have an identity of their own so that they do not blend in or clash with other graphics; a unique colour or style will help them stand out. Text should be clear and simple to read and in a contrasting colour to the background. It is worth noting that lower-case letters are easier to read than capitals.

As much as written information is critical to inform the customer, too much can confuse. A customer will not often have the time or patience to stop and read numerous lines of text. Short, punchy statements can be more effective.

## Pricing tickets

Pricing individual products can be executed in two ways. Some retailers may wish for the price to dominate the product; discount stores and sale items will definitely benefit from this technique. Large stickers or "swing tags" are placed on the items and stacked high to encourage high-turnover sales. Price stickers, although in a prominent location on the packaging, should not cover the brand name. All prices should be in the same place on each item, ideally to the left at either the top or the bottom. A table with multiples of just one product may require only a free-standing sign showing the price.

Retailers who may wish their products to appear more exclusive will benefit from placing price stickers either on the back or bottom of the merchandise. A small, boxed item can easily be picked up and examined for the price; placing the sticker out of sight means the customer has to engage with the product. However, larger or fragile items such as vases are best priced at the back towards the bottom; it is unwise and risky to suggest that the customer handles expensive items.

Garments should have their price tags securely attached, either with a safety pin or by using a kimble gun, which forces a small plastic tag through the fabric with a thin needle. Care should always be taken to ensure that the needle does not destroy or mark the garment. The seam or label is the most appropriate place for the tag to be attached. Trading standards vary in each country: some require that the price is visible on the garment; others are happy for the price to be positioned discreetly inside. It is always worth researching the local trading laws before pricing products.

### Checklist for tickets:

Handwritten tickets will look shoddy and unprofessional.

Always check for spelling mistakes.

Ensure the text is not too long.

Use a clear, simple typeface that is easy and large enough to read.

Use one size of ticket.

Different-coloured tickets for different departments can be effective.

Perspex ticket-holders will collect dust; they will need to be cleaned regularly.

Hanging signs must be secure; an air vent may cause them to sway.

**Above**
The store guide for a department store needs to be simple and easy to read because of the amount of information it has to carry, given that such stores will have many floors to describe. Peter Jones in London is a good example, as shown here.

**Above middle**
On arriving at the foot of the escalator on the ground floor of Peter Jones in London, customers learn more detail of what they will find on the floor. The large "G" and fashion graphic adds instant information as customers descend, with the detail listed beneath.

**Above right**
At the Gap, a ticket is attached to the garment so that it is visible to the customer.

### Printed graphics

The use of printed images will free up a lot of time for a visual merchandiser. Hanging a printed banner with a picture or design on it where a product display is usually housed – or even behind a collection of mannequins – to form a backdrop will create an instant focal point. A major benefit of a printed graphic is that text can easily be added to it, so that not only will customers be aware of the image, they may also be informed by the message.

A graphic refers to a printed image that can be either a photograph, drawing or a piece of artwork incorporating an image and text. Many graphics that appear either in store windows or in-store are connected to a brand's advertising campaign (the brand being that of the store or of the individual designer placed in a store, for example). They are often supplied in a large format that can be incorporated with the brand's shop fit. They are removed and updated seasonally. Modern graphics are usually digitally printed at high resolution by photographic technicians. The cost of printing large banners digitally is minimal compared to the old screen-printing methods. Images can be any size and in full colour, black-and-white or sepia. Printed graphics, when used correctly, can change the appearance of a department or shop dramatically. They are easy to use and easy to store. Adding text to graphics will also send a message as well as look appealing.

There are many reasons why retailers rely so heavily on graphics in-store and in windows. The major rationale is cost. During the 1980s, the cost of producing in-store displays to the same standard and quality as the windows escalated, sometimes way over the set budgets. A simple solution was to use printed backdrops to create the same drama as a display. Often they never matched the more traditional methods. Today, however, they are a much-appreciated tool that is often used with the more conventional techniques of visual merchandising.

**Above**
Large-scale graphics give the appearance that they have fallen at Lane Crawford, Hong Kong. The result is an interesting display with unusual angles created on the store floor.

**Below**
A simple collection of photographs showing Neil Barrett's menswear collection is attached to the wall to highlight the clothing in front, at the Lane Crawford store.

**Above**
An installation for Costume National in the atrium of Lane Crawford, Hong Kong. It was loosely based on its showroom and lasted only one month.

**Below**
Universally, cosmetic counters utilize backlit transparencies to promote their brand and product range, as shown here in a department store in Tokyo.

### Backlit transparencies

Most perfumery counters around the world prove how effective backlit transparencies can be. Simply put, the box that houses the transparency consists of a lightbox with four sides and a row of fluorescent lamps at the back. A Perspex or glass sheet at the front supports the transparency. More often than not, the frame supporting the Perspex or glass will unclip, making it easy for the image to be replaced. The image is produced as a transparency by a photographer and, like the digital graphic, can come in various sizes. Often brands will supply their own transparencies.

Backlit transparencies are cost-effective and very low-maintenance. Once the unit is fixed to a wall, fitting or fixture, it needs little attention. They are a great tool to brighten up a dull corner of a store as well as send an important message to the consumer.

**Above**
A large backlit transparency acts as a focal point to attract customers at Bershka in Tel Aviv.

# Lighting

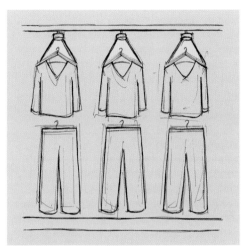

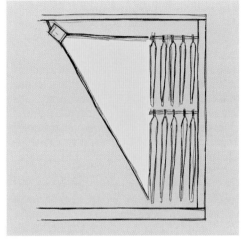

**Lighting plays an integral part in any retail environment, whether it is used for highlighting an in-store focal point or simply to flood the fixtures with enough light so that the customers can easily find what they are looking for (see Lighting chart on page 219). On no account will lighting be the most economical item on the visual merchandiser's budget; good-quality, effective lighting fixtures can be expensive.**

Unfortunately, retailers do not always utilize lighting rigs to their full extent. Many still place all of their efforts into dressing the display, yet fail to make it stand out with the use of good lighting. Often the most exciting visual areas in a store are hidden in the shadows.

A track system with adjustable lamps offers the most flexibility for in-store displays and gives the visual merchandiser the opportunity to use several different lamp fittings, each of which will perform a different role within the display. Spot fittings will highlight an individual piece of merchandise, while flood fittings will give an ambient light to the whole.

The wattage and beam width of a lamp can be baffling to a novice. The actual lamp fitting is useless without the correct lamp. Many lighting fixtures can house a variety of lamps, but not all of them will be universally effective. The size of the beam width you require usually depends on the size of the grouping it is expected to highlight. A small product item such as jewellery, for example, will only require a three-degree beam width; anything wider will illuminate the surrounding area. Shop floors are often lit with fluorescent strip lighting that, when used properly, gives an overall ambient light that is both effective and efficient.

**Lighting should never be an afterthought. The following should always be considered when creating a display:**

Does the display lend itself to lighting?

Is the display in an area accessible to electrical sockets or a lighting track?

How will the display be lit?

What fittings are required to light the display?

**Above left**
When lighting a wall, lights should be adjusted so that the beams are focused on the clothes and not on empty adjacent walls, floor or ceiling. The lamps should always face the wall and should not be directed into the shop, blinding the customers.

**Above right**
The correct-sized beam width should be used: anything too small will highlight just one section of a garment; anything too wide will spill over the presentation.

# Case study:
# ERCO lighting

**ERCO lighting was established by Arnold Reininghaus in Lüdenscheid, Germany, in 1934. Today it is still a family-run business, with an enthusiasm for and philosophy about lighting rather than business. Nevertheless, it operates successfully around the globe, with offices in more than 60 countries and over 1,000 employees. Working with such luxury retailers as Chanel, Burberry and Prada, ERCO is noted for its professionalism and innovative lighting-design technology.**

Jeff Griffiths, the company's Retail Lighting Sales Director, is responsible for implementing ERCO's lighting in many of the world's premium stores. He talks passionately about the use of lighting in the retail sector.

### How do you decide which lighting system to use within a store?

"Each area within a store needs a different lighting treatment, because they have many different purposes and will serve many roles. It is important to have an understanding of how lighting can be used to set an ambient mood as well as to highlight product. Some stores still struggle with this concept."

### Window lighting must be challenging. What are the key principles for lighting a window display?

"The windows of a store are the portals to the brand, and the customer interface, so it is important that they are attractive and eye-catching. Most windows are viewed from an angle as the customer approaches them. This problem might be counteracted by a fashion store, for example, by using a narrow-beam spotlight to highlight specific products rather than flood the whole window with light. By using this technique one is able to create an intimate view of the product, which will be surrounded by darker pockets.

Spotlights are traditionally clipped to a lighting track mounted on the ceiling of a store window. Generally, to produce an effective lighting scheme they should be placed 1 m (3 ft) apart across the width of the window. The lighting track should be at the front so that the spotlights can be directed into the window and focused on the product. A second track can be attached to the centre of the ceiling so that lights can be focused on the back wall to create stunning effects, or simply to wash the wall with light. Coloured lighting can add extra dynamism to a window display.

Technology is now used in stores to increase and decrease the lighting in response to sunlight. Stronger lighting is required during the day than at night, because it will have to compete with natural daylight whereas a dark window requires less light. Such systems also save energy."

**Above**
In D&G's London store, directional ceiling-mounted spotlighting highlights the products hung from a rail against the wall, as well as the mid-floor fixtures.

### In-store lighting must vary depending on the store. Is there a retail science behind the relationship between ambience and directional lighting?

"It is important in a store that there is a strong contrast between vertical and horizontal surfaces, because as humans we look ahead in our natural surroundings: 80 per cent of the information we receive comes from vertical surfaces. The common mistake retailers make is to shine lights down from the ceiling and highlight the floor. Showcasing the floor is clearly a waste of useful and expensive lighting. Vertical surfaces give depth to a store, and since linear space is essential to frame a department store or smaller store it should be correctly lit to highlight the product displayed against the walls. The exception is mid-floor free-standing fixtures, which also require lighting; a series of spotlights mounted in the ceiling and directed on to the fixture is sufficient.

Fashion stores require different styles of lighting because they have many roles to fulfil. For example, a group of mannequins will require directional spotlighting to highlight them, whereas mid-floor fixtures will require a wider beam of light to frame them. The access light spilling into the walkways creates a virtual corridor that can be used to lead the customer through the store.

Cash desks must also be considered when the lighting scheme is designed. Not only should they be highlighted within a store so that the customer can identify them from a distance, but also this is the consumer's last chance to see their chosen items wrapped and packed. One seldom looks at the sales assistant – all eyes are on the precious purchase – so the counter should be well lit."

**Above**
A mannequin has been spotlit in the window of the department store de Bijenkorf in Amsterdam. The intense light counteracts the natural daylight.

**Below**
Uplighters are incorporated into the architecture of the Duvetica store in Milan, while directional track fittings highlight the puffer jackets hanging from a rail.

### How do you decide which lighting system would benefit a retailer?

"I like to meet at a store and ask the client to watch the customers shop. Observing whether they look at the windows and the product displayed can highlight a lack of effective lighting, since that can make customers show little interest. We then do a store walk and discuss what could be done to improve the overall lighting, and how the merchandise would benefit from better lighting. Most clients do listen and take on board my recommendations, but budgeting often hinders improvements."

### Lighting the exterior of a store must be challenging. How does it work?

"Exterior lighting is paramount. A store may be glossy inside but dull on the exterior. Technology is so advanced that we can change the colour of the outside of a building using lighting that can be controlled from a smartphone or tablet. The use of LED lighting means that at the touch of a button the whole facade of a store can change colour in matter of seconds. We can create store logos that rotate on the pavement, encouraging the customer to enter the premises, simply by adhering a laser-cut stencil to the front of a spotlight."

### Are there lighting trends?

"Retailers are now moving away from flat, bland lighting that spills across the whole shop floor towards more atmospheric lighting that highlights a brand or sub-brand by using different levels of lighting to create a specific ambience for their product."

### You must have creative constraints, such as budgets. Does this frustrate you as a lighting expert?

**Above**
A mixture of overall ambient lighting and spotlights is used at the Kiton store in Milan. The bust forms have been spotlit with a higher intensity to ensure that they stand out, to help promote the product.

"Lighting is often secondary when planning a new store, partly because retailers are not experienced in the technology and systems required to enhance a store's ambience. They are, however, familiar with store fixtures! The fear of the unknown and of cost implications can intimidate them. Lighting is a major design factor that should not be overlooked, and should be included in the overall store design."

### ERCO is clearly successful because of its innovation. Which project was the most challenging?

"ERCO has worked with many retailers across the world. One that comes to mind is the Burberry flagship store on Regent Street in London. The whole project took a year to complete, with over 900 light fittings designed specifically to enhance the windows and in-store environment."

**Above**
The use of spotlights in Lanificio di Tollegno and Ragno in Milan highlight the product, not only on the walls but on the mid-floor fixtures too.

**Below**
Uniqlo's flagship store in New York relies on consistent overall floodlighting without directional spotlights. The back walls of the alcoves in which the mannequins stand are light boxes, and highlight and frame the displays.

# Ambience

## Music

The visual merchandiser's role often might not stop at laying out the shop floor and ensuring that the store is presentable and promoting the brand image. Today, it is likely that visual merchandisers will also be called upon to look at the overall level of the store's ambience and atmosphere. They may be asked to decide if music should be played while the customers shop, and if so, what they should be listening to.

Music undoubtedly will add ambience; however, it is wise to consider which music suits the style of merchandise and the customer. A loud din of contemporary music may be off-putting to an older lady shopping for curtains, while it might inspire a younger audience browsing in a denim shop. It may also be sensible to check that the lyrics are not offensive.

## Aromas and scents

Aromas and scents will stimulate the senses of shoppers – provided that the customer likes the smell. Atmospheric aromas can also be introduced to an area that warrants them and can help to promote a product. Scented candles displayed in an aromatic environment will boost sales.

Some aromas are linked to their product category, particularly if that is an item of food, but it is always best to ensure that items are fresh. Nasty smells will, of course, be off-putting; disguising them will only act as a short-term solution. The aroma of freshly baked bread in a bakery will entice the customer to spend, yet the smell of stale fish in a fishmonger's will not have the same effect (the only solution would be to ensure that the fixtures and fridges are cleaned regularly). It is always wise to localize aromas to areas where they can be monitored and amended.

**Conventional visual merchandising may not always be enough to get the overall ambience of the store right. Retailers worldwide strive to offer their customers experiences that are not just merchandise-led. Interaction with a DJ or the tasting of food are just two of the experiences that today's customer now expects.**

**Above**
Anthropologie, London, takes floral decorations to the next dimension, with a vertical garden that spans two floors and acts as an impressive backdrop to the atrium.

For years, department stores have toyed with the idea of pumping aromas through air-conditioning systems to please shoppers. This idea, however, has never been proven to work. Everyone's senses are different; what one may like, another may loathe. In an extreme case, a customer may be allergic to an alien smell – with genuinely distressing consequences.

## Plants

Plants are a great way of creating ambience, colour and even scent. All will need watering, but outdoor plants will need to be placed outside for periods to make them last.

**Above**
An oversized toadstool acts as an impressive eye-catching centrepiece in the ACNE store in Los Angeles. The bright red stands out against a backdrop of cold, neutral metallics.

**Below**
Customers are encouraged not only to shop at Selfridges in London, but also to enjoy a film at the Everyman cinema temporarily installed there.

# Technology

**There is constant pressure for retailers to incorporate technology into the design of their stores. Not only is it important in enhancing the customer's experience, but also it is seen as a status symbol and a demonstration of a brand's innovation.**

Traditionally, customers shopping in a store would have been aware of technology only at the point of sale, when paying for their goods using a debit or credit card or cash. Today, technology is prevalent throughout the store, and not only with the predictable screens promoting products or reinforcing advertising campaigns. Many supermarkets expect the consumer to scan their own groceries to speed up the payment process and reduce the staff payrol (an "unexpected item in bagging area" is an annoyance that we are now all too familiar with). The traditional information board that helped with navigating the store is being replaced with interactive screens that let the customer scroll through the list of available products and brands (although there is a danger that the customer's search will be hindered by children who see the screens as large games consoles). Many retailers extend their offer on the shop floor through interactive screens, where space allows. Samsung has introduced touch screens that the customer can use to plan their living space, including of course the latest Samsung products, without the assistance of a salesperson, giving the individual the freedom to play – with an added expense at the end.

In 2012 Burberry opened its flagship store on Regent Street in London. The unique selling point that drew media attention was not only an impressive shop fit-out, but also the use of technology. An extremely large flat screen showing current catwalk collections was positioned in the centre of the store as an anchor feature to inspire the customer to buy

**Above**
At its flagship store on Regent Street in London, Burberry has embraced technology by using a large flat screen to show not only its current fashion shows but current bands that it supports.

into the brand. When certain outfits were lifted from a rail, the screen automatically showed the complete ensemble, giving the customer the chance to see how it looked on a real person.

The rise of the smartphone and tablet, and the fascination with social media, meanwhile, have made the shopping experience virtual. Social media has introduced a whole new vocabulary: we now take "selfies" on our smartphones; "like" pictures, updates and comments; and abbreviate words into text language (the last usually by removing vowels or using acronyms). In 2014, when his much-anticipated first British store was opened, Karl Lagerfeld – unlike most design-ers, who are protective of their couture masterpieces – encouraged his fashion followers to take "selfies" using wall-mounted tablets while trying on his clothes in the changing rooms. The customers could then share their images with friends all over the world. This clearly indicates the power of social media and the reach it has across the globe. Marketing teams are no longer required to produce print campaigns; the Internet has made marketing instant, and easy to edit and update at the push of a button.

The smartphone is no doubt the retailer's preferential twenty-first-century platform. Shoppers will always enjoy the thrill of browsing in a store, but now they can be reminded of purchases they failed to make. The smart technology iBeacon, which is used in stores across the globe, including Macy's in New York, recognizes the customer's buying history and sends a message to their smartphone to inform them of items they have missed or advise them of offers. As they enter a store they are identified by the chip in their phone, and their valuable personal data is captured.

Until the turn of the twenty-first century the shopping experience began at the threshold of the store; today it starts online. Consumers begin their journey by researching the item they wish to purchase, comparing prices, availability and delivery options; some may simply look for store locations and opening times. A retailer's website is paramount in engaging the shopper, especially if they are a potential new customer. While navigating a website an individual is able to discover not only the products and brands available but also the history of the store and its policies, including its commitment to sustainability and the environment.

With the constant threat of online retailing, the ambience of a store is more important than ever. Retailers work harder and harder to devise concepts that make the selling space innovative and unique. It is not uncommon to find an electronic mirror that projects the selected clothes on to the body, instead of requiring the customer to endure the hassle of actually trying them on in the confines of a fitting room. Even traditional-style fitting-room mirrors are now often designed to enhance the shopper's features through strategic lighting.

The future of retail is to use a smartphone to make a purchase while in store but not at the cash desk. The customer may be guided around the store by an app or an actual person, but the paying method will be theirs to decide. The Japanese, noted for their fascination with vending machines, have been at the forefront of fingertip purchasing for decades, and the concept has more recently been developed elsewhere in the world. The launch of interactive window screens by such companies as the food giant Tesco hit the headlines because of its innovative technology, but it remains to be seen whether they are much used. It is not yet clear whether Tesco has expanded this concept beyond Asia across the globe, or whether it is a simple marketing tool designed to create media interest and demonstrate the retailer's futuristic thinking. The new innova-tion in retail delivery is click and collect. Customers can now browse the Internet, make their purchases online and have their items delivered to a secure location close to their home. Local stores and even railway stations will now receive the packages, store them and wait for the customer to collect them.

Technology may be at the forefront of retail, as brands strive to be at the leading edge of store design, and it will certainly increase consumer spending. However, it is important to question whether such a resource can be overused and seen as gimmicky. Today's equipment is affordable and easy to access and use, but retailers must consider whether the consumer, while shopping, might feel

overwhelmed by interactive screens and
constant updates on their phone about
missed opportunities. The simple, tried-and-
tested attributes of a store's ambience are
often the most effective – "energy" from the
customers, engaging sales assistants,
atmospheric music and scents, and innovative
presentation of product.

**Above**
A traditional bust form dressed in a
Burberry Mac stands in front of the
large flat screen in the Regent Street
store.

# Retail standards and maintenance, and budget

**The importance of maintaining the visual standards of a store or a shop floor should never be underestimated. Enlisting the help of the sales team can dramatically affect the workload of a visual merchandiser. Training the sales staff to implement a basic level of visual merchandising that can be easily utilized will be a long-term benefit. A visual merchandiser, for example, may not require the sales associates to create displays or dress mannequins, but they can assist with the everyday merchandising of the fixtures.**

## Standards and maintenance

Most retailers will expect their shop floors to be neat and tidy, ready for the morning trade. Producing a booklet to explain how to maintain the visual merchandising standards is an effective way of communicating the requirements to the sales associates. A generic layout can be used and then updated easily each season. Weekly training sessions conducted on the shop floor by a visual merchandiser with the sales staff will also help clarify the roles and responsibilities of staff. Giving individual ownership for specific product categories or brands will also help build a visual merchandising structure within the sales team.

### Stock replenishment

Stock replenishment is best done while the store is closed, either in the evening or first thing in the morning. Managers and owners of prestigious stores do not generally allow trolleys and running rails on the shop floor during opening hours. This discipline should be practised in any retail environment. Customers should not be distracted by anything but the merchandise on offer.

### Housekeeping

Housekeeping should also be completed while the store is shut. Walkways and aisles should be cleaned and cleared of any obstructions. Fixtures must be dusted and cleaned. Garments should be refolded or hung, remembering to ensure all the price tickets are still attached. Dirty or soiled product should be either cleaned or replaced.

### Cash desks

Cash desks must appear professional at all times and be uncluttered and user-friendly. Customers, especially when parting with large amounts of money, do not expect to see scribbled notes and family pictures taped to the till. Clean and tidy flat surfaces should also be allocated for folding garments before they are placed into a carrier bag.

## Budget

The budget for in-store visual merchandising also requires some thought. When ordering fixtures and fittings, the choice can be between bespoke items or those bought directly from manufacturers. The latter will often be the most economical but possibly not the most inspirational. Fixtures should, however, be seen as an investment; unlike a window scheme, they will have a longer retail life. When planning an in-store floor layout, budget money should also be set aside for additional lighting, graphics and signage, which are often overlooked. A hard-wearing floor may also add additional costs to the overall project but, in the long term, will be cost-effective.

# Virtual visual merchandising

For many years, visual merchandisers have had to rely on a sheet of graph paper and a pencil to draw out their floor plans. Today, however, technology is available that makes the process of creating a floor layout or designing a store quicker and more effective. Various computer programs can be used to create a "virtual store". Used in tandem with the buying and merchandising functions, these programs can hold libraries of merchandise that is, or will be, in-store at any one time. Such virtual products can be dragged and dropped onto fixtures that are also part of a separate library that the visual merchandiser can either build or import from suppliers' catalogues.

First, walls and floors are created to scale, and then bespoke colour schemes can be added. Once the fixtures are in place, the products can be hung on rails, or folded

items can be placed on shelves or tables. The complete store design can be viewed as either a plan or an elevation, and with some programs the user can take a three-dimensional tour of the space. Lighting can also be directed to the relevant fixture and adjusted to give an even more realistic point of view. Mannequins, signage and graphics can also be added to create in-store displays.

The computer programs are by no means inexpensive, but in the long run they can be cost-effective because of their versatility. With just a few days of professional training, and even more of practice, they can be used to produce excellent-quality visuals.

**Above**
A computer program by MockShop showing the overall layout of the virtual store. It offers the ability to generate a plan for each fixture, including each item's style or colour, unit and location of each fixture, along with the appropriate signage.

MONDA
CASUAL

FORMAL

CASUAL

WORKWEAR

5th March 07  WEEK 12  11th March 07

### Store communication: design directives

Worldwide, multi-chain retailers as well as the individual brands themselves continue to give importance to brand identity and want to ensure a consistent brand message and experience for the consumer in all stores. To achieve this, the visual merchandising function now extends as far as corporate headquarters, where a unified vision is created and disseminated to the stores in the form of design directives.

Directives generally follow either a vertical or horizontal path. Retailers like Gap create design directives at the corporate level. These highlight key seasonal trends and include: window displays; hot shop displays found immediately inside the store entrance, featuring the latest trends of the season; departmental displays that focus on the consumer end-use; and floor plans for an A – B – C store-level hierarchy, where A stores do the highest volume of sales and carry the full collection, and other stores do less volume and carry limited groups from the collection. Directives are sent to individual shops (the process is known as vertical dissemination), where staff are relied upon to carry out the directives in each outlet. District and regional managers frequently visit these stores to make sure directives are correctly implemented in a timely manner.

Brands often supply retailers with branded fixtures to create in-department branded areas. Regardless of whether they provide branded fixtures, however, vendors also create directives containing information about seasonal advertising, trends and collections, with suggestions for merchandise placement. Some vendors may rely on store staff to implement these directives (horizontal dissemination).

Many retailers and brands are investing in proprietary trade software to integrate their merchandise management and stream-line their operations. The value of these programs is that they allow designers, merchandisers and retailers to work and communicate visually. This is a great advantage, since 90 per cent of all information input is visual.

US brands such as Levi's, Calvin Klein, Tommy Hilfiger and Dockers, and retailers such as Macy's and Dillard's have chosen British-based Visual Retailing to provide an integrated suite of software programs that includes storyboarding, assortment planning, analysis, collection building, database management and fixture design as well as visual merchandising in the form of VisualStore, also known as MockShop.

**Above**
MockShop allows the visual merchandiser to create a floor plan for the store, either digitally or via hard copy, to communicate the design directives.

### The virtual store

The retail outlet is modelled in three dimensions, with all the components of the brand image and collection represented. The physical shop materials selection (i.e. floor materials, paint colours, etc.), windows, signature or branded fixtures, in-store signage, as well as merchandise are combined in three-dimensional views for ease of merchandising at retail level. When a retailer elects to use Visual Retailing, VR representatives work with the company to build a variety of "libraries": fixtures, store decor, and interior materials (flooring, paint, etc.). The retailer enters its items, signage and mannequins into a seasonal database.

Using drag-and-drop technology and a series of libraries, visual merchandisers can determine the size and configuration of the space and assign flooring, wall and ceiling coverings. Working in a combination of plan and 3D views, they drag and drop fixtures from a library and arrange them on the selling floor. Each fixture contains a "connector", a "container", or a combination of the two, which allows merchandise to be placed on the fixture. Connectors place hanging items on fixture bars and arms, while containers automatically fold garments on shelving or flat surfaces, or accept graphics. Merchandise can be moved from hanging to folded areas or vice versa, and the program displays them in the correct mode. The number of units assigned to each arm, bar or shelf can be increased or decreased.

Once the floor merchandising is complete, the visual merchandiser can then prepare images of various views of the store and fixtures for use in the design directive. An individual fixture plan that details the items and their placement can be generated as well. Finally, an overall statistics report for the floor plan can be created, detailing item information and retail value in a spreadsheet format, with a final calculation of projected sales per square or linear foot.

Directives can be created in the "visual storyboard": a page-layout tool that is useful for creating mood, inspiration and collection development communications. As information is updated and changed in any area of merchandising – for example, changing a colour or style – the updates are automatically

reflected throughout. Because of its visual approach, Visual Retailing is easy to use once you master the icons, shortcuts and processes necessary to complete the tasks.

Design directives are generated several times each year to coincide with seasonal collections and delivery. For example, fashion apparel often includes autumn, spring, holiday and transitional seasons. Design directives would be generated for each of these.

**Design directives are seasonal design guides that include some or all of the following information:**

Overall seasonal trend information, advertising, fixtures and other general miscellaneous information.

- - - - - - - - - - - - - - - - - - - - - -

An overview of how the merchandise category works across collections or classifications (i.e. shoes, lingerie, etc.).

- - - - - - - - - - - - - - - - - - - - - -

In-depth information by collection or classification, such as a possible "theme", key colour, textures, fabrics or styles, display ideas, fixture flow and categories and floor plans, and any other notes specific to the merchandise category.

**Above**
Further features of the MockShop program offer visual storyboards for key items (top), windows (middle) and fixtures (bottom).

# Store study: Topshop

**The worldwide fashion phenomenon Topshop is part of the Arcadia group, owned by retail guru Sir Philip Green. The brand has grown from strength to strength over the last decade and as a result has a presence in more than 20 countries. The flagship store in London's West End boasts a nail bar and a hair salon among the 8,400 m² (90,000 ft²) of the season's "must-have" fashion labels.**

**The company's collaborations with up-and-coming as well as established designers has made the brand a desirable destination for fashionistas. Its most high-profile collaboration saw British supermodel Kate Moss designing seasonal collections to sit within the brand. As well as showing high-street collections at London Fashion Week, Topshop has expanded its business outside the UK, and now has stores in the USA, South Africa and Australia.**

Tim Whitmore, Topshop's creative director, started his visual merchandising career dressing windows on London's King's Road. He has worked for some of the UK's most successful high-street retailers, including Selfridges, Warehouse, Wallis and Miss Selfridge. In 2009, Whitmore won the Visual Merchandising and Display Award, for the second time, for his ongoing contribution to the world of creative retailing. Whitmore is a respected member of London's visual merchandising community.

**Topshop is a retail victory; clearly the windows play an important role. Do you have a favourite window scheme that you designed?**

"When I look back at the windows I have designed and installed over the years, it is always the simple ones that stand out. I am always excited about developing new window schemes; as with everything in life, your creativity evolves with time and new ideas occur and inspire."

**What, in your opinion, makes a good window display?**

"Something that is so clever, or produced to such a high visual standard that it stops you in your tracks. And, of course, a window

**Above**
The Topshop store in New York opened to much acclaim. The fashion-forward British brand was hailed as a huge retail success.

display that makes you want to enter the store and see more of the merchandise that is available."

### Once the windows are planned and installed, how do you bring the Topshop theatre in-store?

"I always have a theme or concept in mind for every new seasonal collection, which comes from working closely with the design team.

In the seasonal theme, I have many different window ideas that my team and I develop in order to see what will work visually. The in-store drama derives from the overall theme that I develop with my creative team for both 214 (London's flagship store) and the regional stores: we often trial some elements of the flagship store in a smaller store before we place orders for props for all of the smaller stores."

**Above**
Brightly coloured rosettes sit in front of a British Union Jack backdrop, while a dramatically posed mannequin sits amid the Topshop collection.

**Above**
An impressive collection of shoes is backlit, with yet more lighting in the form
of chandeliers. Vintage furniture takes on a modern twist.

### In-store displays take up valuable selling space. How important are they to promote the Topshop image?

"The amount of space in-store displays demand is dependent on the size of the store and in which city it is located. In our major city stores these areas are very important as they create a 'wow' factor and demonstrate how different we are from our competitors, and they obviously add to the whole experience and ambience we create for Topshop."

### Do fashion trends inspire how your in-store displays look?

"Absolutely!"

### Are mannequins still an important tool that you use to inspire your customers?

"Yes! Very much so. We have mannequins, bust forms, torsos, etc., in all of our stores, but we use different specifications and ranges in different stores, again depending on the size, turnover and city location. We use high-quality mannequins from Schlappi and Rootstein in our city stores all over the world. We also use ranges from Planet, Universal and Panache in other stores. In all our stores our mannequins have bespoke wigs and stylized make-up especially designed for Topshop. Our mannequins are always fashion-forward and have innovative looks inspired by the seasonal trends."

### How often do you re-merchandise the interior of a store?

Every day we remerchandise the sales floor, depending on sales and deliveries, to keep the departments fresh and exciting.

### Topshop New York has received rave reviews. Was it difficult to get across the strong British retail concept to the Americans?

"Not at all! The New Yorkers love Topshop. It was great fun to work on this project – hard work but great fun. The store looks amazing."

### How important was the store design in making the whole shopping experience successful?

"The success of this store, like any store, relies on a few major factors that are equal in their contribution: the store design, the creative overlay, the in-store visual merchandising, and of course, the store team, but the most vital element of any successful store is the product."

### Where does your creative inspiration come from?

"Life, and living in a great, vibrant city: London. Being able to travel anywhere in the world for inspiration is vital for me as a creative individual, but it is also coupled with a combination of the arts, media, theatre, music, fashion, books, magazines and friends."

### Which store do you admire?

"I love the new Louis Vuitton Maison store in New Bond Street, London; Dover Street Market for the products; as well as the Comme des Garçons store in Tokyo."

### You recently won the Visual Merchandising and Display Award for Best Display Person in London for the second time. What advice would you give to anyone wanting to follow in your footsteps?

"Work hard and get involved in everything. If you have a passion for this industry and you work hard, you will progress. It always helps if you are creative first, but also have a commercial side to you. Being a team player is hugely important."

### Your creativity does not stop at the windows. How many tattoos have you got and what percentage of your body has been embellished?

"When I am asked this I always say, 'One tattoo; it's just very large'. My tattoos actually cover nearly all of my body – I think about 85 per cent. I have stopped having my body decorated; I think it's time to stop now before they look too much but, then again, I think I may have already crossed that line!"

# Mannequins

"Mannequins are very much in vogue today. Fashion is not just about the clothes anymore; it's about the hair and make-up, too – the complete look. What better tool than a good mannequin to get a fashion statement across to the masses? There was a trend in the 1980s to try and use other props to carry clothes; garments were hung on broom handles; headless torsos and blow-ups of artwork were all tried but were not necessarily as successful."

Kevin Arpino, former Creative Director, Adel Rootstein Display Mannequins

**Mannequins have been the trademarks of window displays for decades. They are the most effective tools you can use to present the latest fashion trends. Some customers aspire to look like them, and visual merchandisers often form a friendship with them. Many individuals still do not realize that these fibreglass showroom dummies are in fact modelled on actual people.**

Adel Rootstein Mannequins is the world-renowned manufacturer of mannequins. With two new collections added to its vast range every year, its mannequins are bought and used by retailers worldwide. Adel began her career in 1956, making wigs and supplying display props to the retail trade from her kitchen in London. Being aware of the growing social and fashion trends of the early 1960s, she began creating models of London's style icons. Her first major mannequin was a cast of the 1960s' fashion model Twiggy. Later models included Jodie Kidd, Joan Collins, Sandie Shaw, Joanna Lumley, Karen Mulder and Yasmin Le Bon, to name but a few. Her legacy lives on, and today's visual merchandisers trust her mannequins to help realize their creative displays.

Kevin Arpino has been fundamental in driving Adel's business empire. As creative director, he is responsible for selecting whom to immortalize as a mannequin, building collections and dressing them in his legendary unique style for the many Rootstein showrooms worldwide.

Although mannequins have been fundamental to window displays in stores globally, it is worth noting that mannequins have not always been so fashionable. As Kevin Arpino explains, "In the fifteenth century, mannequins were made to represent the Madonna; they were carried through the streets of Europe as part of religious festivals. In a way, even then they were designed to carry clothes. The early Madonnas were made from papier mâché and leather and were very primitive-looking. The French can be credited for refining the mannequin. In the 1800s, the Parisian House of Worth produced mannequins that were an extension of the forms used for making clothes. Often they were used to emphasize the trend of the day and they had nipped-in waists to show corsets and bustiers.

"The mannequins of the 1920s looked more contemporary because they were fashioned in the style of the period: Art Deco. Fashion designers were keen to show their creations on a torso that was 'of the moment'. Adel should really be credited for introducing commercial mannequins that were fashion-forward and inspiring. She was very aware of the growing ready-to-wear collections that had a higher turnover than the couture costumes. Mannequins needed to look younger; the mannequins before the swinging sixties resembled someone's mum!"

**Above**
Grouping mannequins is a skill that takes a long time to master. Deciding which two work together and how they should be positioned often depends on the strength of the outfits and their poses.

**Opposite**
A collection of Adel Rootstein mannequins that have been dressed and arranged to show how they can be used in-store. Each pose is carefully considered so that the garment will be shown to its full advantage.

# Sculpting

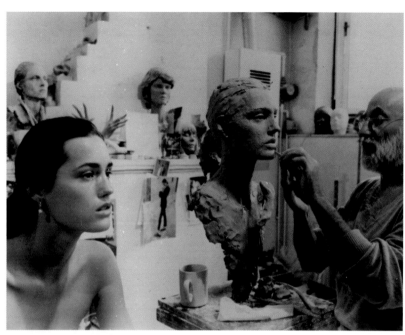

working as a mannequin that Rootstein changed and adapted the collection to suit her style.

As a popular and successful company, Rootstein constantly needs to update its collections. As Kevin Arpino explains, "I start putting ranges together by ascertaining what we and the customer require. During the 1980s, for example, many stores were ripping out their windows to give the customer a view of the store. Mannequins that had once been viewed through a sheet of glass were then suddenly scrutinized by customers in-store; the hair and make-up needed to be refined. Retailers also saw the potential of using mannequin forms in-store to promote their merchandise; headless forms painted white were used against sparse white walls so that the clothes stood out, and the mannequins became part of the design and architecture of the store. The more dramatically posed and dressed models stayed in the windows.

"We also have to take into consideration the nature of the retailers' business. If they have a boutique selling couture, they might require a dramatic, elegant pose that suits the product they are showing. Retailers on the high street may require a more simplistic pose, and sports shops might prefer an action mannequin. It is also important to remember that not everyone has the skill to dress a mannequin with a striking pose; often the Saturday girl with no experience will be challenged with the task of dressing the windows – a simple collection with no striking poses that are difficult to dress will always be beneficial. We have around 500 different mannequins in our range, many of which belong to collections. A collection is generally made up of 12 models that are designed to interact with each other if used well."

**A mannequin begins as a clay sculpture; most mannequins are modelled on real people. At Rootstein the model sits for the sculptor for a two-hour sitting every day for three weeks. The sculpting is done in the traditional way by placing the wet clay onto a wire armature. The hands are the only part of the body that is cast from life. Once the sculpture is finished, the clay figure is cast in plaster. The plaster then becomes the mould for the fibreglass mannequin that is sent off to the shops. The whole process takes three months from start to finish.**

Creating a range of mannequins is time-consuming. Each model must have an individual pose that will sit within the complete collection. On occasion, a model will come to a casting and the whole collection will change because of that. Erin O'Connor, for example, had such a strong idea of how she saw herself

# Purchasing mannequins

**Purchasing a selection of mannequins for a store will provide a range of options to help promote any fashion collection. Whether just one mannequin or a whole collection is required, consideration should be given to what they will be used for, where they will be used and whether their poses will be suitable for the clothing they will be wearing. Remember: a sports-inspired mannequin may not be suitable for an eveningwear collection.**

Mannequins come in all shapes and sizes: from adults to children, maternity to action and stylized to realistic. Before purchasing a range of mannequins, consider the type of business in which they are to be used. A commercial, easy-to-dress range of mannequins that have simple poses will give more flexibility and will adapt to the ever-changing fashion trends. A dramatically posed mannequin may work well in a heavily stylized environment.

The average body size for a mannequin purchased in the UK is 34, 24, 32 (size 10). Plus-size mannequins are becoming more widely available because of controversy in the fashion media; as a result, British department-store chains have started to introduce mannequins in a more realistic size 14.

A range should be selected carefully so that the mannequins can be used individually or grouped to create a family; this might include a selection of standing, sitting, lying and leaning mannequins. It is worth thinking about whether you need more dramatic poses; do remember, though, that an expensive mannequin designed for hanging may be used in one scheme but will not be used for the rest of the year. An extreme pose may also be difficult to dress.

At the same time, consider how long the range will last. A dramatically posed, realistic mannequin can easily be used to promote a fashion-forward look with the right hairstyle and make-up, which can then be restyled from season to season. It is worth bearing this in mind if you are working to a tight budget – you may not need to purchase new mannequins if you can reuse existing ones. You can, of course, also save by purchasing some styles of mannequin that can be used time and time again for one style of garment: a rigid bust form, for example, for a man's suit. An economical range could also be built up from mannequins with no facial features, or even no heads, because they do not require make-up renovations or wigs.

Having said all this, many retailers still prefer just a simple bust form that resembles a torso and will carry clothing without overpowering the garment. These are most suited to men's tailors and classic ladies' fashion stores where, traditionally, stylized mannequins are not used.

The quantity of mannequins you purchase may be costly, but do consider how many are required to create a complete window fashion scheme. Ten windows with three mannequins in each will equate to 30. The interior display sites will require even more, thus adding to the mannequin budget. A range of children's mannequins, on the other hand, will not necessarily fill a large window because of their size. They will inevitably work better as a large group, so this should be borne in mind if you are working in a children's retail store.

Another consideration to be borne in mind is that renovating mannequins can take up to a month; it may be worth having a secondary collection to use while they are out of service, especially if your store only retails fashion. Clearly, while the mannequins are away being renovated, this would be a good time for a department store to install a home-related scheme.

**Above**
The New York socialite Dianne Brill promotes the fuller figure with her range of mannequins.

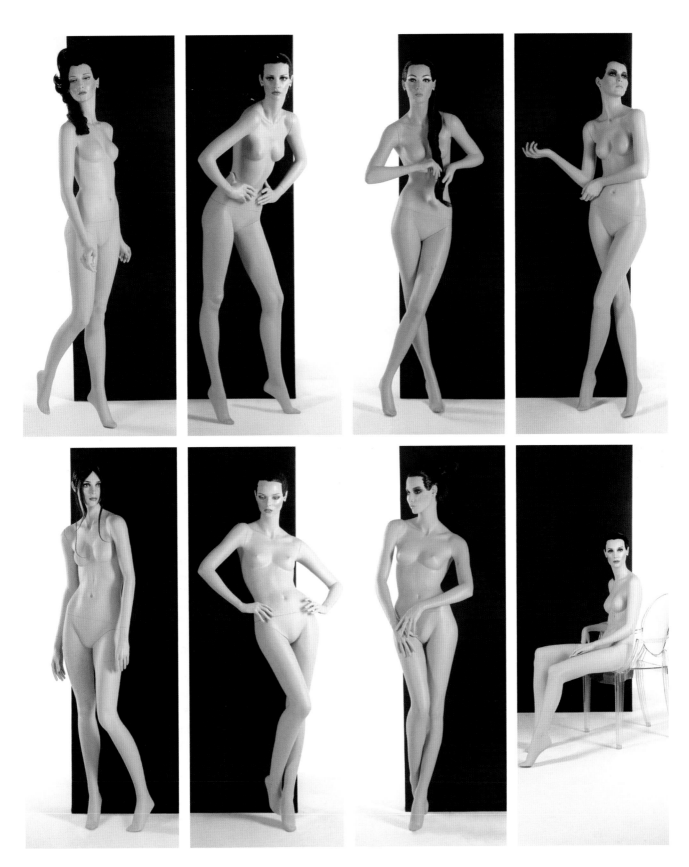

**Above**

A range of mannequins is designed so that they interact with each other. The majority will be standing, but sitting, lying and leaning mannequins are also introduced to break the pace and add interest. Customers can buy complete ranges or individual mannequins.

# Dressing a mannequin

"A mannequin can be a great prop for a display; if dressed badly, however, they can look awful. People do the strangest things to mannequins that they just would not do to themselves. If a dresser is unsure of how to dress the mannequin, [he or she] should keep it simple. Clothes should be given movement; if the model's hands are on the hip, throw the coat over it – don't just let it hang. Pinning a garment is paramount not only to ensure the clothes fit, but also that they look good. A pin should never be seen – a good dresser will pin the inside of the garment. Realistically, a size 14 dress should be pinned so well that it looks great on a size 10 mannequin. When I dress a showroom with over 40 models, I always dress one first of all from head to toe to make certain that I will be happy with the look I am trying to achieve."

Kevin Arpino, former Creative Director, Adel Rootstein Display Mannequins

**Dressing mannequins is not as easy as it appears. Apart from having to disassemble them, they can be very heavy and clumsy, depending on the pose. The end result should, however, look as elegant and as lifelike as possible.**

The dressing of men's and ladies' mannequins can differ; consequently the guidelines on page 193 cover both categories. Children's mannequins should also be categorized by their gender when being dressed. Once you have decided which mannequins are to be used, it is essential to follow these guidelines.

**Above**
A sitting mannequin with a strong pose that will look effective as part of a display, but is difficult to dress if she is to wear trousers because her legs are crossed. Rather than remove a leg, loosen it slightly and pull trousers up and over the knee to the waist.

**Above**
To create movement on these mannequins riding horses in a Harvey Nichols window, London, the skirt hems and other materials have been wired through the seam and moulded to give a lifelike appearance.

**Above**
Before it is dressed, a mannequin can be broken into sections. The hands, arms, waist and one leg from this mannequin are detachable to help dressing. Skilled dressers may not need to disassemble the mannequin completely but loosen some joints.

**Below**
Once dressed, the same mannequin takes on a completely different appearance.

## Dressing menswear

All clothing should be pressed and steamed beforehand.

Both mannequin legs should be secured together and turned upside down, resting on the floor so that the feet are facing upwards. At this stage socks should be placed on the feet and trousers pulled over and down to the waist, ensuring that they remain taut to prevent creasing. Most tailored trousers are unfinished and should be measured, turned up and pinned prior to dressing. Shoes can now be added.

The clothed legs can now be returned to the upright position, and the torso can be fitted back onto the legs.

The upper garments can now be placed around the torso or pulled over the head onto the body. At this point, shirtsleeves should be pulled through the jacket arms, ready for the manne-quin's arms to be fitted.

To fit the arms, remove the hands and carefully push an arm through the layers of clothing down the sleeves towards the cuff. Then secure the arm to the socket on the torso.

The hands can now be reattached to the arms and the mannequin can be placed in its final position.

Now is the time to dress the mannequin properly. Start by ensuring that the trousers are the correct length. Tuck shirts carefully into the trousers.

Loose-fitting garments can now be carefully gathered at the rear of the mannequin, or at the point that is least visible to the public. The excess fabric should be folded inwards and pinned, preferably through the seams to limit any damage to the garment.

The mannequin can now be styled and accessorized, paying attention to detail and finish.

Finally, it is always advisable to view the mannequin from the same direction as the public. Check for visible pins, loose threads and ill-fitting clothes.

## Dressing womenswear

As with menswear, it is essential that all clothing is pressed and steamed beforehand.

The legs should be assembled and turned upside down. If hosiery is required, it should be added at this stage by carefully rolling down and over the legs.

Trousers and shoes should be treated in the same way as for menswear.

Unlike male mannequins, female mannequins will often have different-sized foot insteps. A mannequin with a high instep will require the exact heel height to ensure that it stands upright, while those with no instep will need flat shoes such as a pump.

The mannequin can now be turned upright and should be secured in its final position.

To fit a skirt or dress, turn the legs back into the upright position and attach the torso. On most occasions the garment can now be pulled over the head and secured in place, but often a tight-fitting skirt will have to be pulled over the feet and up to the torso before the shoes are fitted and the mannequin is turned upright.

Top garments can be added and arms attached as for menswear.

Styling and accessorizing can now be completed. This should include pinning, draping and pleating the garment to create an inspirational silhouette.

To begin, take the mannequin to the place where it will be displayed. This should be done with care because mannequins are fragile. Most new mannequins – or newly renovated ones – will be delivered with their limbs and body parts packaged separately. It is best to ensure that you have all the correct body parts before attempting to construct the mannequin. Remember: the limbs from one mannequin are not compatible with another. Many mannequins come with markings on their body parts so that they can be easily matched to the torso, thus making the assembly effortless.

If your mannequin has been in storage, it may need to be cleaned with a light detergent to remove any dust. Attention should be given to the face in particular as this is the area that is most visible. It is sometimes advisable that two people dress a mannequin if it has a complicated pose; one visual merchandiser can support the mannequin while the other dresses it.

"The visual merchandisers at Bergdorf Goodman in New York know exactly how to dress a mannequin, as do those at Neiman Marcus. Both have very skilled dressers that prove how mannequins can add drama to a window display. Zara uses mannequins very well. They realize how they can help sell their product."

Kevin Arpino, former Creative Director, Adel Rootstein Display Mannequins

### Advanced styling for mens- and womenswear

Many experienced visual merchandisers will not stop at using outlandish wigs, make-up and styling. Occasionally they will wire hemlines invisibly to give the garment movement, apply handpainted acrylic nails to the mannequin's hands, and cut and style wigs to suit the overall look. This advanced styling is best noted at prestigious department stores such as Barneys in New York and Harrods in London.

**Rachel Sproule has been dressing mannequins since the age of 17, when she took a job as a junior dresser at London's Harvey Nichols store. Since then, she has taught her skills to various visual merchandising teams at Selfridges and New Look, showing the dedication to mannequin dressing that made her a leader in the UK's visual merchandising fashion circuit. She is now Creative Director of Evans. Her tips are:**

Tape tissue paper to the legs of a mannequin to give volume and movement to a skirt.

Push a couple of pins through the lapel or breast of your shirt/sweater so that you can get access to them easily when pinning a mannequin's clothing.

Shoes can be slid over the feet of a mannequin that has already been spigoted in the leg by easing the weight of the mannequin up but not completely off the spigot. Turn the shoes sideways and slip them on, then lower the mannequin back onto the spigot.

Cushioned wig tape can be applied to the mannequin's head at the front and the sides to help support a heavy wig. Pins can be pushed through the wig and secured into the tape.

If you need to twist the arm of a mannequin from its natural position to hold a handbag, place a large bangle around the mannequin's wrist to disguise the unaligned join.

If a mannequin has not got pierced ears, Blu-Tack can be used to secure clip-on earrings.

Double-sided tape can be used to secure stockings to the legs of mannequins.

If a belt is too large for a mannequin, shorten it to fit by wrapping an elastic band around the excess at the back of the mannequin.

Wannabe make-up artists should leave it to the experts who work on mannequins – professionally. Cosmetics will melt and run; paint will not.

**Above**
A simple bust form is often the best way to display men's tailoring. Here at Thomas Pink, the articulated arms are moved into a position so that the hand interacts with the tie.

# Securing a mannequin

**There are numerous ways that a mannequin can be secured, but there are three universal fittings that are generally used to support a mannequin.**

The first is the foot spigot, which is a round or square metal rod attached to a base plate made from either glass or metal; the spigot is pushed into the foot to support the mannequin. The spigot can also be removed from the base plate and screwed directly into the floor; the downside of the foot spigot is that the shoes will have to be drilled through so that the spigot can go through the sole of the shoe.

To get a mannequin to stand straight and upright on a base plate, gently ease it to the tip of the spigot, place your foot on the base plate to secure it and use the mannequin's height as a lever to bend the spigot to the position required. Finally lower the mannequin back onto the base plate.

The second option, the leg spigot, works in the same way but goes into the calf of the leg, which means that shoes can easily be shown without damaging them. In the US, the last option, the bum rod, is often preferred. A longer rod is pushed through the leg of the trousers or under the skirt and fits into a hole in the bum cheek.

Many skilled professionals use wire to support mannequins. This complicated technique is called "strike". Two wires are wrapped around the waist of the model and firmly secured by twisting the wire around itself, then pulled taut in two opposing directions, ensuring that the mannequin is upright and attached to the floor with nails. The wire is then twisted around itself and the excess is cut off. Once the wire and the nail head are painted the same colour as the background, they become invisible.

When striking a mannequin wearing swimwear or lingerie, ensure that the model wire is secured around the fitting that holds the torso and legs together, and trail the wire through the gap between the two and to the rear of the mannequin or the part of the body that will not be seen by the public. One wire should then be pulled through the legs and the other towards the back and attached to the floor; thus the wire will not be seen around the naked waist of the mannequin.

Keep a selection of Perspex or wooden blocks (which can be painted the same colour as the floor) in various sizes; these can be used to block (raise and support) the heel of a shoe if the mannequin has a high instep. This will also help when striking, ensuring that the mannequin is straight and balanced.

**Above left**
The mannequins in this window from Macy's demonstrate the use of striking. Wire is secured to the back of the waist, is then pulled taut and nailed into the floor panel. Wires can then be painted out using the same colour paint as the background.

**Above right**
Three mannequins on an in-store display are stabilized using base plates. A metal spigot is attached into the leg so that the shoes are not damaged. A foot spigot would go through the sole of the shoe.

# Grouping mannequins

**Most mannequin ranges are designed so that they can be positioned in an aesthetically pleasing way. They are often developed to interact with each other. Badly positioned or grouped mannequins can have a detrimental effect on the overall creative appearance of any display.**

Grouping models is a skill that will create something that is gratifying for the customer to look at. A line of ten models may not be inspirational; it may be better if they were positioned to interact with each other. A window with six mannequins should also be broken up into groups, such as a group of three, two and a solo figure. Ideally there should be only a couple of overstyled stars in the window; the other mannequins should support them.

Mannequins wearing trousers should be positioned behind ones wearing skirts so that they do not block the skirt; short coats should be in front of long ones. At the same time, you can take advantage of these groupings to help the customers understand the different clothes used in the window or display. A suit that comes with either a skirt or trousers can be shown easily on a group of three mannequins, demonstrating all of the options, and the group can be given cohesion by carrying accent colours onto the other models.

**Above**
It is important that mannequins interact with each other. Even the eyes should always focus on something, such as another mannequin, to create a more lifelike appearance.

# Maintenance

**Mannequins should be well cared for and kept clean. A simple felt body bag can be used to cover them when they are in storage. Dirty, chipped mannequins will not help sell any clothes. Once a mannequin has been purchased it can be resprayed and have new make-up applied; in the trade this is referred to as a "reno". Kevin Arpino describes the process: "Mannequins come back to us. We start by stripping the face of the make-up. We then take off layers of the base paint, fill any cracks and respray them. Finally, we create and apply new make-up. A full renovation face and make-up costs around £80 ($130), whereas a new mannequin would cost between £700 and £1,000 ($1,125 and $1,600).**

"Wigs are also an economical way of changing the mannequin's appearance. We offer two wig options: hard and soft hair. Both options will cost between £60 and £100. A hard wig is styled and set so that it will keep its shape and not move. They can be extremely dramatic but not very versatile. Soft hair resembles a more conventional wig that can be styled by the visual merchandiser."

Mannequin dressing is an art that many take very seriously. Visual merchandisers take a lot of pride in styling their muses. Often they use their experience to leap into the fashion world as stylists. Kevin Arpino, an advocate of mannequin dressing, believes it is a dying skill that should be studied and practised. "Those fashion dressers that aspire to dressing the world's top models for an eight-page shoot in *Vogue* should remember they are only as good as their address book," he says. "Their first job as a stylist may be to dress someone to resemble a grandma for a washing-up liquid commercial. Styling a mannequin can be more rewarding. At least they don't question what you are putting them in."

**Above**
A dramatically posed mannequin supports this elaborate couture coat, which has been wired through the hem to give the impression of movement.

# The Visual Merchandiser's Studio

**To some visual merchandisers, a studio can be a luxury; to others, it is a necessity. Large established department stores have always allocated a space, either in the flagship store or away from the retail environment, where visual merchandisers can plan and create their windows and in-store displays. Depending on the needs of the visual merchandiser, this valuable accommodation can include complete workshops and even dummy windows that can be used to test future window schemes and displays.**

Costly to run and maintain, many of these in-house studios, unfortunately, have been converted into selling or storage space. Much of the work that they used to produce is now contracted out to props specialists. However, a visual merchandiser lucky enough to have the space and staff to run a studio will benefit from having the equipment listed below.

### Office space

For organizing and designing and the storage of files and drawings.

### Product preparation space

A clean and dust-free area where products can be stored before or after they go into a window. Running rails should also be installed for garments and shelves for fashion accessories.

### Ironing and steaming

A professional iron and ironing board and an industrial steamer are necessities for prepping fashion items.

### Workbench

This should be large enough to take a 2.4 x 1.2 m (8 x 4 ft) sheet of wood. The bench should be sturdy with a fixed wooden top.

### Spray booth

A designated area should be allocated for a spray booth that has adequate ventilation; most spray paint is extremely toxic.

### Sink

A large sink with hot and cold water.

### Tool cupboard

A metal storage cupboard that can be locked will protect valuable tools.

### Plan chest

A large plan chest is the most efficient way to store plans and visuals.

### Cupboards

Separate storage is needed for spare lighting fixtures and lamps, to hold cleaning equipment and for paints, brushes and cleaners.

### Ticket holder shelf or cupboard

Perspex ticket holders will scratch if not cared for. A designated shelf or cupboard will help keep them in good condition.

### Ample electricity sockets

Rather than running the risk of causing an accident by trailing extension leads across the studio, electricity sockets should be housed near the areas where power tools will be used.

### Industrial vacuum cleaner

A domestic cleaner will not be sufficient.

### Overhead lighting

Efficient lighting that gives a good overall light.

### Extractor fans

Ventilation for both paint fumes and sawdust.

# The visual merchandiser's toolbox

**Any visual merchandiser will benefit from having a comprehensive selection of tools. The actual toolbox should be large enough to house the tools, but not so big that it becomes a burden and takes up a vast amount of valuable window space. Windows can be confined and sometimes claustrophobic – the more compact the toolbox, the better. Items the visual merchandiser will need are listed below.**

## Staple gun

Probably, in conjunction with a pair of scissors, the most important tool that a visual merchandiser needs. The staple gun has many roles, including for covering floors and wall panels.

## Staple remover

These small specialist tools are the only effective way of removing staples easily.

## Pliers

To remove panel pins and stubborn staples.

## Scissors

The trademark scissors protruding out of a back trouser pocket often identify a visual merchandiser.

## Double-sided tape

Useful for quick repairs and fixes.

## Pins

As well as traditional dressmaking pins, stronger pins that are more durable and can be hammered into wooden surfaces are used. Dressmaking pins should only be used to pin garments.

## Hot-glue gun

Excellent for major repairs.

## Screwdrivers

Both flat-head and posidrive. An electrical screwdriver is also a useful commodity for changing plugs and fuses.

## Bradawl

Useful for boring holes.

## Retractable tape measure

A long measure that stretches the length of a window is more effective than a shorter one.

## Spirit level

Useful for ensuring any picture or graphic is level.

## Wire

There are many different gauges of wire available. A selection of galvanized, florists', model and thin wire will be sufficient.

## Selection of screws and nails

A mixture of nails, including carpet tacks, panel pins and masonry nails, will be needed for different purposes. Wood and masonry screws together with the complementary size of rawplugs will help if you are screwing into a stone or a wooden wall.

# Health and Safety

The responsibilities of a visual merchandiser may differ from day to day, so take time to analyze how best to implement any health and safety standards as early as possible.

**Health and safety should always be taken seriously. Visual merchandisers must ensure that any public space they are working in is kept clear at all times. When working in a confined or isolated space such as a window, they must also ensure that they adhere to health and safety disciplines.**

**There are three areas within a store where visual merchandisers should consider both their own and the public's safety: the studio, windows and store interiors. Listed below is a health and safety checklist for each of the areas:**

## Studio

Power tools should be used with the correct protective clothing: i.e. eye shields and gloves when required.

Electrical apparatus should not be used near water.

Do not attempt to move heavy props by yourself; they will often require two or more people to manoeuvre them.

Spray paints and strong adhesives will require adequate ventilation.

Electrical cables trailing across the studio floor can cause accidents.

## Windows

Ensure all power tools are used with the correct protective clothing.

Many visual merchandisers prefer to dress a window without any footwear on to ensure that they do not ruin or mark the floor. Care should be taken, however, not to step on nails or staples.

Speakers connected to the store's public address system should be installed in isolated windows to keep the visual merchandiser informed of any need to evacuate the store.

Ladders should be firmly secured before use; it is advisable to have one person stabilizing the bottom while another climbs.

Lighting tracks should be earthed and wired in professionally.

Never cut corners when wiring lamps, etc. Always ensure the correct fuse is used with the correct plug.

When using toxic paint, it is advisable to make sure that the window is well ventilated. It is often best to leave the window open while the paint is drying.

## In-store displays

Mannequins must be secured properly: on many occasions children will want to play on them.

Ladders must only be used with another person stabilizing them. This will ensure stability for the user as well as informing the customers that the ladders are in use.

Electrical cables must not trail across the shop floor at any time.

Sharp or electrical tools should never be left unattended.

Painted items must be dry before they are placed where customers will come into contact with them.

## Fixtures

Any fixture used to hold merchandise must be secure and stable.

Shelves must be secured and strong enough to take the weight of the merchandise. Shelves should never be overstocked.

Any undressed fixture can be hazardous for customers; empty garment prongs or arms can be dangerous. It is always advisable to remove the prong or leave at least one item of clothing on the end of the arm or prong while remerchandising the display to ensure that customers are aware of a potential hazard.

# Lighting chart

| Lamp/bulb | Voltage/fitting | Location | Suitability |
|---|---|---|---|
| Fluorescent tube lamp | High-voltage | Overhead fittings, frequently ceiling-mounted | Non-directional; efficient; used to provide high-level overall lighting in stores |
| Tungsten/incandescent filament | High-voltage | Overhead lighting, table and wall fittings | Commonly used in domestic environments; often used for secondary lighting in retail outlets |
| Tungsten/incandescent strip light | High-voltage | Under-shelf lighting, picture lights, floor lights | Non-directional; provides a softer light output than fluorescent tubes |
| Tungsten incandescent reflector lamp | High-voltage | Used with specialist fitting, in windows, in-store and outdoor fittings | Directional light output for high-lighting specific areas of a display |
| Crown silver tungsten/ incandescent cap lamp | High-voltage | Used with specialist fitting with adjustable reflector | Window lighting and some interior displays; can be easily focused |
| Halogen capsule lamp | High- or low-voltage | Window lighting and interior display, used with specialist fitting with adjustable reflector | Highly efficient; adjustable; ideal for focal-point directional lighting for displays |
| Halogen dichroic lamp | Low-voltage; used with specialist fitting frequently containing a transformer | Window lighting and interior display | Sealed 1-amp for window and interior lighting, available in several beam widths. Excellent for general displays and creating theatre |
| Metal halide lamp | High-voltage | General lighting used for window and in-store displays | Harsh, efficient strong light, low-maintenance; takes time to reach full light output capacity |
| Fibre optic | Low-voltage | Small display cases, effect lighting | Excellent for jewellery or similar products because the light unit can be housed remotely. Fittings are small and discreet, although with poor light output |
| Light-emitting diode (LED) | Low-voltage | Low light output cold-running lamp for close proximity lighting such as showcases | Poor light output. Available in several colours; unsuitable for general display lighting as it cannot be focused |
| Low-voltage cold cathode | Low-voltage | Similar to neon in appearance used in store signs and display effects | Available in many colours; excellent for building excitement; can be located in areas accessible to the public |
| High-voltage neon | High-voltage | Outside signs and effect lighting | Must be professionally installed and expensive to maintain; not suitable for interior signs |

**Above**
This chart gives the description and the ideal uses for the various lamps available in conjunction with the correct light fitting.

# Glossary

**A**

**Accent lighting** The use of lighting to emphasize displays or merchandise units

**Adjacencies** Deciding which products sit next to each other on a floor plan or layout

**Ambient lighting** Overall lighting used in-store

**B**

**Balance** Visual weight

**Banner** Printed text or graphics, often suspended from the ceiling

**Barriers** Fixtures used to block customer flow

**Base plate** Metal or glass plate that houses the fixture (spigot) that supports a mannequin

**Beam (lighting)** The light projected from a lamp

**Brand awareness** Understanding the brand and its mission statement

**Branding** Communication tool used to enforce a designer, store or product

**Bust form** Torso of a mannequin, often without a head, designed to display tops only

**C**

**Capacity fixtures** Units designed to carry fast-selling items

**Ceiling grid** Metal structure fixed to the ceiling of a window or interior display

**Chevron** Arranging fixtures at 45-degree angles to encourage customer flow

**Closed window** Window with a back wall

**Colour-ways** The colours manufacturers have chosen to use in their fashion or home collections

**Concession** Another brand bought into the host store

**Cross-merchandising** Pulling non-conventional products together to create a display or hot shop

**Customer flow** Manoeuvring the customers through the store with ease

**D**

**Display base** Raised platform used in-store to create display on

**Diwali** Indian festival of light

**Dressing** Styling a window, grouping or mannequin

**F**

**Face-outs** Fixture components used to show the full front of fashion items

**Fixture density** How much stock a fixture will or should hold

**Flagship** The main store of a large retail company

**Focal points** Areas that stand out

**Folding board** Cut piece of wood or cardboard used as a template when folding clothing

**Footfall** Number of customers entering a store or department

**G**

**Gobo** Design burnt out of metal through which light is beamed to create a logo or design that is projected onto a surface

**Gondola** A four-sided fixture used primarily for home or food products

**Graphic** Printed picture often used as a backdrop to a display

**Grid wall** Metal wire wall fixture system

**Grouping** Product displayed to create interest

**H**

**Hot shop** Area used to display promotional or themed merchandise

**K**

**Kimble gun** Tool used to fix price tags to a garment or fabric product

**L**

**Layout** Placing and arranging products and product categories on the retail floor

**Lightbox** Backlit box that houses a transparency

**Linear** Retail wall space

**Logo** Name of brand used to enhance display

**Luxury retailer** Designer brand

**M**

**Merchandise** Product on sale

**Mid-floor fixture** Product fixture that is placed away from the wall, should be shopped at 360 degrees

**Multiple sales** Encouraging the customer to purchase more than one item

**O**

**Open-back window** Window without a back to it

**Optical weight** How products used in a display balance visually

**P**

**Prepping** Preparing product beforehand for a display

**Price point** The retail price of the selling items

**Props** Items used to enhance a display as part of a theme or scheme

**R**

**Reno** Renovation of a mannequin

**S**

**Scheme** The overall idea and concept of the display

**Shop fit** Design and construction of the interior of a store

**Showcase** Miniature enclosed window used for smaller displays

**Sight lines** Use of fixtures to draw the eyes' attention

**Signage** All forms of ticketing or text used in-store or in windows

**Slat wall** Slatted panels that attach to a linear wall that supports rails, shelves and prongs to hold merchandise

**Spigot** Metal pole that supports a mannequin either through the foot, ankle or backside

**Striking** Use of wire to support a mannequin

**Swing ticket/tag** Price or informative ticket attached to the product, often with a kimble gun or string, ribbon etc.

**T**

**Text** Written words used on a sign

**Theatre** Creating excitement within the retail environment

**Theme** The use of a creative window scheme running through the windows to create a story

**V**

**VM** Abbreviation of visual merchandising

**W**

**Wall fixture** System used on a retail wall to hold various fittings

# Further reading

## Books

*New Retail*
by Raul A. Barreneche
(London: Phaidon, 2005)

*Silent Selling: Best Practices and
Effective Strategies in Visual
Merchandising*
by Judith Bell and Kate Ternus
(New York: Fairchild, 2002)

*Big Ideas for Small Retailers:
Discover New Ways to Improve Your
Business* (Paperback)
by John Castell
(Cirencester, Gloucestershire:
Management Books 2000, 2006)

*Collidoscope: New Interior Design*
by Nigel Coates
(London: Laurence King, 2004)

*Store Window Design*
by Aurora Cuito (ed)
(New York: TeNeues, 2005)

*Fashion Retail*
by E. Curtis
(New York: Wiley Academic, 2004)

*Contemporary Visual Merchandising
and Environmental Design* (5th edition)
by Jay Diamond and Ellen Diamond
(Upper Saddle River, New Jersey:
Prentice Hall, 2006)

*Retail Buying* (8th edition)
by Jay Diamond and Gerald Pintel
(Upper Saddle River, New Jersey:
Prentice Hall, 2008)

*New Retail*
by Rasshied Din
(London: Conran Octopus, 2000)

*Smart Retail: How to Turn Your
Store into a Sales Phenomenon*
by Richard Hammond
(Upper Saddle River, New Jersey:
Prentice Hall, 2003)

*Design for Shopping:
New Retail Interiors*
by Sarah Manuelli
(London: Laurence King, 2006)

*Applied Visual Merchandising*
by Kenneth H. Mills, Judith E. Paul and
Kay Moormann
(Englewood Cliffs, New Jersey:
Prentice Hall, 1982)

*Window Display: New Visual
Merchandising*
by Tony Morgan
(London: Laurence King, 2010)

*Wonderwall: Masamichi Katayama,
Projects*
by Shigekazu Ohno
(Amsterdam: Frame and Basel:
Birkhauser, 2003)

*Visual Merchandising and Display:
The Business of Presentation*
by Martin M Pegler
(New York: Fairchild, 1983)

*Powershop: New Japanese
Retail Design*
by Carolien van Tilburg
(Basel: Birkhauser, 2002)

*Retail Success: Increase Sales,
Maximize Profits, and Wow Your
Customers in the Most Competitive
Marketplace in History*
by George Whalin
(San Marcos, California: Willoughby
Press, 2001)

## Magazines

*Creative Review*

*Frame*

*FX*

*VMSD*

## Websites

*www.bonaveri.com*
Mannequin suppliers

*www.elemental.co.uk*
Props and visual merchandising
solutions

*www.fashionwindows.com*
Online fashion and window information

*www.hindsgaul.com*
Mannequin suppliers

*www.lectra.com*
Virtual visual merchandising

*www.morplan.com*
Store equipment supplier

*www.patinav.com*
Mannequin suppliers

*www.proportionlondon.com*
Mannequin suppliers

*www.rootstein.com*
Mannequin suppliers

*www.shopfittingsupplies.co.uk*
Shop equipment supplier

*www.superfuture.com*
Worldwide stores

*www.universaldisplay.co.uk*
Mannequin suppliers

*www.visualretailing.com*
Virtual visual merchandising

# Index

# Picture credits and acknowledgements

## Picture credits

The publisher would like to thank the following picture sources:

Courtesy Acne: p185 top; AFP/Getty Images: p175 right; Alexander McQueen, Milan, William Russell/Ed Reeve: p32 bottom; Alexander McQueen, New York: p148; Anthropologie: p184; Apoc, Paris/ Ronan and Erwan Bouroullec: p75 bottom; Baccarat, Paris/Claude Weber: pp35, 36, 139; © Benoit Florençon: 128; Bergdorf Goodman: 108; Bershka: pp52 top right, 178; Bisazza, Berlin/Alberto Ferrero, www. albertoferrero.it: pp30–31; Courtesy Burberry, London: pp186–9; Camper: 116–17; Image courtesy Canoe Inc.: 37; The Chicago History Museum: p13 top; Colette, Paris: pp29, 161; 10 Corso Como/Vanni Burkhart: p123; Debenhams: pp165–166; Dover Street Market, London: pp138, 145, 155; www.edgedesignfit.com Design and Implementation by EDGE Design Fit Ltd (all images are © copyright protected): p143 top; Images courtesy Erco: pp180–3; Courtesy of Flight 001, New York: pp156–7; Fortnum & Mason, London, visual presentation by Paul Symes: pp21, 112, 114 top; Fortnum & Mason, London, visual presentation by Paul Symes /Andrew Meredith: pp 66 bottom, 73, 90, 106, 113, 114 bottom, 115; French Connection, London/Andrew Meredith: pp79 top, 104; Globus Food Hall, Zurich: p160; Halfords/© Pentagram/Harry Pearce: p174 top right; Harvey Nichols, London/Michael Taylor: pp8–9, 10 bottom (window by Thomas Heatherwick), 60–1, 98, 107, 207;

Heal's, London/© Pentagram, Domenic Lippa: p174 top left; Hulton Archive/ Getty Images: p10 top; Photo courtesy and © 2014 Isetan/Mitsukoshi: p12; Courtesy of IT Beijing Market: p34, 119 top; J Sainsbury plc: p174 bottom; Courtesy of Karl Lagerfeld: 137 bottom; Kurt Geiger/Found Associates/Guy Archard: pp42–5; Lane Crawford, Hong Kong: pp20, 23, 119 bottom, 164 top, 169 left, 176, 177 top; Last Footwear: p28; Liberty, Great Marlborough Street, London, by Maxine Groucutt, in collaboration with Laura Tarant Brown/Andrew Meredith: p71; LL/Roger-Viollet/TopFoto: p11 top; Louis Vuitton/Stéphane Muratet: pp 91, 96–7; Macy's, New York, p70 bottom, /Paul Olszewski: p211 left; Courtesy Maison Martin Margiela: pp135, 169 right; Matthew Williamson: pp 130–3; Maxstudio, Los Angeles/LA eyeworks/Fotoworks: pp52 top left, 143 bottom; Carlo Moretti: p137 top; Nike: pp53, 149, 163 top; Oleg Nikishin/Getty Images: p177 bottom; Courtesy and © John Ong: p38; Orange/Giancarlo Gorassini Abacapress.com: p142 right; Peter Jones, London/© Pentagram, John MacConnell: p175 left and centre; Prada, New York/Armin Linke, www. arminlinke.com: p32 top; Pret à Manger: p167; Primark: p122; Printemps Departmental Store, Paris, Eva Glele/Francis Peyrat: pp13 bottom, 16 top, 57 top, 69, 80–3, 88; Prints, Singapore: p142 top left; Ray Tang/ Rex: p16 bottom; Rootstein Display Mannequins: pp7, 99, 198-9, 200, 201, 202, 203, 204, 205, 206, 208, 212–3; The Royal Borough of Kensington and Chelsea, Family and

Children's Service/John Bignell: p15; Saks, Fifth Avenue, New York: pp41, 93, 164 bottom; The Selfridges Archive held at The History of Advertising Trust Archive: p11 bottom; Selfridges, Birmingham/Future Systems / Soren Aaagard: p33; Selfridges, London/ Andrew Meredith: pp2, 14, 17, 18–19, 25, 46-49, 51 top, 52 bottom, 54, 57 bottom, 58–9, 62, 64-5, 66 top, 78 top, 84, 86, 89, 94, 100, 101 top, 109, 127, 140, 147, 168, 185 bottom, 210, 211 right, 214–5; © Shopics/Alamy: p136; Stella McCartney, London/Ed Reeve: p129; Stella McCartney, New York/© Frank Oudeman, www.frankoudeman.com: p51 bottom; Supreme, Los Angeles/ Harry Allen & Associates/photo by Hage: p141; Topman, London: pp63, 144; Topshop, photos by Melvyn Vincent, Michael Taylor, design consultants: Dalziel & Pow: pp27, 56, 70 top, 72, 95, 101 bottom, 102, 163 bottom, 194–6; Courtesy of Tsvetnoy, Moscow: p162; Uniqlo, Tokyo/Nacasa & Partners Inc: pp105, 150; Urban Outfitters: p67; Visual Retailing Software Distribution Ltd: pp191–3; Vittorio Zunino Celotto/Getty Images: p39; VV Rouleux, www.vvrouleaux.com: p142 bottom left; Windowswear: pp 171–3; Zara/INDITEX S.A.: p26.

Illustrations by Majka Zylinkski, revised by Carolyn Hewitson: pp55, 74, 77, 78 bottom, 79 bottom, 87, 121, 124, 125, 126, 134, 151, 152, 153, 154, 158, 159, 179.

## Author's acknowledgements

My special thanks go to:

All at Laurence King Publishing – Helen Evans, Anne Townley and Susie May. Peter Kent for the pictures and Majka Zylinski for the illustrations. The UK and US reviewers – Prof. Marie Aja-Herrera, Elisabeth Jacobsen, Janine Munslow, Anthony Parsons, and in particular Anne C. Cecil, Instructor, Design & Merchandising, Westphal College of Media Arts and Design, Drexel University, for her contribution on virtual visual merchandising.

Today's players that push the boundaries of visual merchandising and also agreed to be interviewed – Erin Thompson at Coach, Linda Hewson at Selfridges, Rebecca Farrar-Hockley at Kurt Geiger, Richard Found at Found Associates, Joe Cotugno at Bloomingdales, Franck Banchet and Eva Glélé at Printemps, John Gerhardt at Holt Renfrew, Paul Symes at Fortnum & Mason, Mark Briggs at Saks, Brad John and John Sencion at Flight 001, Tim Whitmore at Topshop, Faye Mcleod at Louis Vuitton and Janet Wardley at Harvey Nichols, Jeff Griffiths at Erco lighting and Tom Phelan at Colorset.

Andrew Meredith – retail photographer extraordinaire!

And finally, my friends and family; Harvey Sutton and Susanne Tide-Frater for their support and loyal friendship and complete dedication to fashion retail.